"Everyone talks about the importance of change in big abstract terms. Jellison shows you how to make change happen in one-on-one relationships."

—Kevin W. Gentry, Ph.D., Vice President,
Lieberman Research West

"The very practical ideas in Jerry's book have been of direct benefit to many of our three thousand member CEOs."

—Bill Williams, President, CEO,
TEC—An International Organization of CEOs

"I've never encountered such an optimistic and constructive approach to managing people."

—Henry Sanchez, Vice President,
San Diego Trust and Savings Bank

"Great! I no longer have to be the office shrink, crying towel, or the heavy to get people to do what I need them to do."

—John Craddock, President, The Savannah Corp.

"If you think you have heard it all before, then this fresh new approach is for you."

—Edward Matthews, Vice President, William Penn Printing Co.

"Have all your managers read this book, and pray that your competitors don't."

—William E. Craycraft, Director, Management Development,
General Instruments Corp.

"You *can* change the leopard's spots. Jerry Jellison explodes the conventional wisdom about how much and how fast you can get people to change."

—Dr. John Blanche, Vice President, RHR International

"Field tested and field proven, Jellison makes sense, without any psychological nonsense."

—Archie Bray, Managing Partner, The Bray Group

"Veteran executives and novice managers will find this book invaluable."

—Bill Renison, P.E., Maintenance Superintendent,
Unocal/Molycorp

Overcoming Resistance

A PRACTICAL GUIDE TO PRODUCING CHANGE IN THE WORKPLACE

JERALD M. JELLISON

SIMON & SCHUSTER
New York   London   Toronto   Sydney   Tokyo   Singapore

SIMON & SCHUSTER
Simon & Schuster Building
Rockefeller Center
1230 Avenue of the Americas
New York, New York 10020

Copyright © 1993 by Jerald Jellison

DESIGNED BY BARBARA MARKS
Manufactured in the United States of America

3 5 7 9 10 8 6 4 2

Library of Congress Cataloging-in-Publication
Data
Jellison, Jerald M., date
Overcoming resistance : a practical guide to
producing change in the workplace / Jerald M.
Jellison.
p. cm.
1. Organizational change.   2. Organizational
behavior.   I. Title.
HD58.8.J44   1993   92-37024
658.4'063—dc20   CIP

ISBN: 0-671-74949-8

For my daughter, Jeneen

Contents

3. Trade Secrets *60*

Discover the trade-offs that transform inequitable relationships into relationships that are equitable and profitable for you and the other person.

4. The World's Most Persuasive Communication *83*

Two little words do all the work of persuading people to change and, with the right timing, they will bring you the results you want.

5. Your Hidden Motivational Resources *101*

Most managers are unaware of the hundreds of resources they already possess that can be used as incentives to get other people to change. From granting small requests to bending the rules, you have a treasure trove at your disposal—regardless of your position in your organization.

6. A Field Guide to Resistance Tactics *125*

Learn to recognize the various tactics people use to resist change—from making excuses and empty promises to getting emotional and calling you names.

II. SIX SIMPLE STEPS FOR GETTING RESULTS *147*

7. Laying the Groundwork *149*

How to prepare for any encounter so that the resistor's defensiveness is transformed into receptivity to your request. The World's Most Persuasive Communication will help you.

8. How to Face Resistance—And Win *162*

Here are specific techniques for each type of resistance you encounter. You'll learn how bambooing, postponing extended discussion, and reinterpreting the other person's reaction can turn persistent resistance into action.

9. The Bottom Line *188*

The one technique to use in those rare cases when all else fails. Plus, you'll learn how to conclude the discussion in a way that minimizes future resistance.

III. YOUR ACTION PLAN *211*

10. Making Change Happen *213*

Here's how you can immediately put these ideas to work. Now you are prepared to take on even your most troublesome problem cases.

Introduction

Have you ever considered asking someone to do something and then said to yourself, "Why bother? It'll just turn into a battle. I'd rather avoid the hassle and do it myself."

If your answer is yes, then you have met a resistor and lost. This is exactly the train of thought the resistor wants you to follow. Anticipating that it will be too much work to get Michael, your production manager, to rewrite his report, you don't even bother asking. Good old Michael doesn't have to change the way he does things, and guess who rewrites the report.

The problem of individual resistance to change is becoming more critical than ever as the pace of change in business accelerates. With downsizing, mergers, new management philosophies, and new technologies transforming our workplaces, we're all putting in longer hours and being asked to do more with fewer people. The stress can be overwhelming, and even the best of workers will sometimes dig in their heels.

Faye is a star salesperson and, wonder of wonders, she's a team player, too. You suggest she take a new territory and, after asking a few questions, she goes along with your request. You ask her to train some new hires, and she gladly does so. Most of the time, people are like Faye; they'll usually go along with you if you simply ask.

But what happens when you ask Faye to begin using a portable computer to communicate her sales call reports by 5 o'clock each Friday? She starts gabbing about the new product line. You restate your request and explain the importance of this computerized information. Now Faye says she'll give it a shot, but nothing happens. When she comes into the office Monday morning, you emphasize how important it is for you to get her information promptly at the close of work each Friday. She promises she'll do it this week. She doesn't.

The following week, you tell her bluntly that you want her reports by Friday at 5 o'clock. Monday arrives, and you still don't have the information. When you go to her office, she begins spouting excuses, and the exchange becomes heated.

You've asked Faye politely three or four times, and she still hasn't changed her reporting method. Faye knows what you want her to do, she knows how to do it, and she knows why you want her to do it. But instead of cooperating in her usual manner, she resists your requests for change.

Managers are caught in the middle of this tension between change and resistance to it. They are being pressured by their superiors to implement more changes, but they must deal with employees who have reached the point of resisting anything new. In the face of this opposition, managers are discovering that their typical methods of leadership and communication no longer produce results. The inadequacy of old techniques makes the need for a new approach especially urgent.

Overcoming Resistance gives you a simple and effective method for solving the problem of persistent resistance to change. It offers *specialized* tools designed for this specific problem, and is not designed to be applied to all employees in all situations. Most of your management practices are very well suited to people like Faye, who are usually quick to comply with your requests. For the special situation of persistent resistance to change, when you find that your usual approaches aren't working, you can use these specialized techniques.

The starting point for producing change in the face of persistent resistance is to revise the way we look at people and why they do what they do. Most management advice relies on traditional psychological interpretations of people and problems. Too frequently this traditional analysis not only fails to solve the problem, it is pessimistic about ever solving it. The implicit assumption always seems to be that, over the course of their lives, people get fixed into rigid patterns that are very difficult to change.

Popular psychology usually teaches us to label problem people. We call them bulldozers or passive-aggressives, and we are led to believe that these psychological monikers will help us cope. We develop different styles of communication for each personality type. But have you ever wondered why the problem people are assumed to be rigid and unchanging, while you are supposed to be endlessly flexible? Why is it always you who has to change?

The approach described in this book differs radically from those traditional assumptions. It assumes that each person, rather than being locked into some stereotyped pattern, is richly complex, and capable of a wide repertoire of actions. You can tap that capacity for change without sending the employee to the psychiatrist's couch or winding up there yourself.

You may find that some of your own management practices and closely held beliefs about human behavior are challenged by this fresh perspective. If what you are doing now isn't producing the kind of change you want, this new orientation just could provide the solutions you have been looking for.

The approach is extremely optimistic about the possibility of producing change in even the most resistant of employees. Of course, you must decide whether you want to expend the energy to make the change. If you determine that it's more cost-effective to terminate, transfer, or otherwise work around the employee, then by all means do so. But don't resort to those costly alternatives until you've given these new techniques a try.

In many situations you can't simply banish the people who are causing problems. You also can't always afford to keep accommodating your work life to their preferences. In such cases this new approach will not only demonstrate that it is possible to overcome resistance to change, it will provide you with concrete tools you can use immediately to make those changes happen fast.

Tools
for
Change

CHAPTER ONE

A New Look at People and Change

From every forum, experts admonish us to thrive on chaos, accept change as part of daily life, and learn to live with it. Those of us charged with bringing order out of chaos and implementing all this change may see the necessity for change, but we live with another reality. People fear and resist change at almost every turn.

We ask someone to do something differently, to improve, to change their approach. They respond with excuses, arguments, tears, a glare, or mute silence. We react with anger or emotional outbursts. These exchanges often escalate until we're swinging a sledgehammer to drive a tack.

As the frustration mounts, we consider farming the problem person out to some unwitting manager. If we can't transfer him, what about threatening his livelihood? If that doesn't get the change we want, we may actually prepare the dreaded pink slip. Worst of all, if we can't change him, transfer him, or fire him, we resign ourselves to the status quo and devote our precious energy to working around this human impediment.

In any organization, you'll find people who have resisted change so effectively that they have secured their own inviolable turf. Their supervisors, co-workers, and subordinates have given up trying to get them to change. They reluctantly accept that that's just the "way he is" and work around him. Other people pick up the slack for the person's obstinacy. Someone else does the detailed paperwork. Someone else handles customer relations. Someone else assumes the task of training the work group in the new personnel policies. Too often, that someone is you. You end up doing another person's work so the job can get done.

THE LIMITS OF POPULAR PSYCHOLOGY

Despite extravagant claims to the contrary, popular psychology has done little or nothing to solve the practical problem of producing change. In fact, traditional psychological thinking usually compounds the problem. It reinforces the notion that change is virtually impossible.

The psychology we've all learned teaches us to typecast everyone around us. We identify the reclusive engineer as an introvert. The hard-driving guy in sales is aggressive. The older male manager who calls the secretaries "the girls" is a chauvinist. The management trainee who keeps asking the boss to check her work is insecure. We end up categorizing people we're having trouble with as snipers, steamrollers, and exploders. The labels imply that the individual is likely to behave the same way in almost every situation. We assume the person is fixed, and we believe people consistently fit their labels. They always have been this way, always are this way, and always will be this one way.

A basic tenet of popular psychology is that people are profoundly influenced by their early life experiences. Years of living have then served to reinforce these early experiences until the patterns become rigid, and by the time we encounter these people in the workplace, they've supposedly been immutably shaped. We all acknowledge the wisdom of the old saying that, as the twig is bent, so grows the tree.

Unfortunately, this implies that what we've got left to work with is deadwood. Changing the shape of these petrified stumps is going to be very tough. We've been told for decades by popular psychology and management "experts" that people behave as they do because of their attitudes, values, and beliefs, because of their personality, because of their needs, motives, or wants, because of their emotions, or because of the level of their self-esteem.

Arnold isn't producing. How do you explain that? The guy's got an **attitude.** He doesn't **value** hard work.

How about Jack, the bane of every woman in his department? Obviously, his chauvinism is the result of his entrenched **belief** that men are superior to women. Of course, we know where he acquired that belief because we know his past. Jack is from an earlier generation, raised in a male-dominated household, and went on to spend ten years in the military.

Why can't the marketing people get along with the engineers? Classic **personality** conflict between the extroverts and the introverts.

Susan just isn't **motivated** to work. She has no **desire** to succeed, and doesn't even **want** to do a good job.

Jane is running a popularity contest instead of her department. She won't say no to anyone because she **fears** being disliked. She's extremely **insecure** and has a high **need** for approval. This is probably because she was the baby of her family, always got a lot of attention, and had very little responsibility. The opposite rationale, curiously enough, is offered as equally defensible. She was the oldest child, much was expected of her, and her parents withheld their praise when she didn't meet their expectations!

Don, the prima donna with whom headquarters blessed you, has a lot of talent coupled with an amazing lack of tact. Why is he so demanding and so inconsiderate of the people around him? Some will say his behavior is caused by his colossal **ego**. Others will say that behind his brash manner is a crippled sense of **self-esteem**.

Led to believe that the only way to change people is to learn how attitudes, personality, needs, feelings, and self-esteem cause behavior, we set out to become psychological experts. Our quest has spurred an entire psychological-training industry dedicated to helping us solve our people problems.

We take tests, and require potential employees and old hands alike to take tests that will reveal their true personality characteristics. We trust these tests to assess management style and ingrained modes of thinking, and to identify who should or should not be promoted. We answer all the crazy questions. Did your mother love you more than your father did? Would you rather read a story or tell one? We dutifully add up our scores and graph out the totals so we can see our profile and learn which labels apply to us. By the time we're done, we're convinced we know who's judgmental, who's perceptive, who's creative, who's analytic, who's emotionally closed, and who's got low self-esteem.

Behind this psychological saturation campaign are some very limiting assumptions and depressing implications, all based on the premise promoted by Sigmund Freud that the cause of present behavior lies in the past. This pessimistic assumption is so widely cherished in our culture that challenging it may seem like heresy. But just watch how it affects us.

As manager of branch operations, one of the people you oversee is named Paul. He runs his neighborhood branch with all the precision and sensitivity of a drill sergeant training new recruits. Not one woman has made it into the officer ranks under Paul's management. A few frustrated female employees are now complaining to upper management. Before the company is hit with a lawsuit, you decide to get this guy to change his management style.

Before you meet with Paul, you try to analyze and understand him. Notice your own train of thought and the kinds of questions you ask yourself concerning Paul. Seeking to understand and alter current behavior, we usually seek out all manner of detail about a person's past.

Where did Paul grow up? What regional and ethnic factors influenced his early life? In what decade did he mature? What were the economic circumstances of his childhood? Was he an only child? If he had siblings, what was his position in the birth order? Did he have strong male modeling? What was his mother's role in his upbringing? Was there co-dependence?

We undertake an intensive study of Paul's past, looking for clues that will help us understand his present behavior. We gather all of these details on the assumption that, because Paul has behaved this way for years, he's probably going to behave this way for years in the future.

If we believe that people consistently behave in predictable patterns, regardless of time and circumstance, then the extrovert will routinely be outgoing and talkative, the introvert will keep to himself, and the person who grew up during the Great Depression will constantly worry about money and practice extreme thrift. All of this implies that change is going to be difficult at best, and most likely impossible. If it took years of shaping to create and rigidify a person's psychological makeup, it is going to take many more years of revisiting and resolving his early life traumas before any significant change can be achieved.

In today's fast-paced, high-pressure business environment, this analysis does little to help us solve our problems. Thinking in terms of attitudes, personality, needs, feelings, and self-esteem provides colorful descriptions of people, but when we attempt to put the reams of psychological profiles to work, we can see how they fall short. What have you gained by knowing that the chronic complainer has a negative attitude, the chauvinist has an entrenched belief that men are superior, and the reckless guy on the production floor doesn't wear goggles because he doesn't value safety? An employee's personal history is of little practical use to those of us who must solve our people problems quickly and constructively, and who must at the same time meet deadlines and bottom lines.

Proponents will argue that once you know the psychological cause of a problem, you can attack it at the root and solve it. But can you? How many deeply entrenched values have you changed in the last six months? If we think that the conflict between sales and engineering is the result of clashing personalities, what solution does this analysis offer us? It tells us that to eliminate the conflict we have to change the personalities. Changed any personalities lately?

This solution is really no solution. Experience has taught us that changing someone's personality is almost impossible. If you have a co-worker with an insatiable need for attention, are you in any position to try to fill that bottomless well while trying to fulfill your job obligations? If you know your boss has a strong need for control, do you have any idea how to get her to give up control over any but the most trivial matters?

Many conscientious managers have attempted to become psychological experts. They pride themselves on their ability to categorize people problems and trace out the historical causes of the problems. But seldom does the identification of the psychological roots and causes help to create change in the workplace. In fact, it serves the self-interest of those people who are objecting to change, who want to maintain the status quo. The notion that people get formed into unchanging patterns benefits the resistors.

Resistors are not a class of people or a kind of person. As used here, the term "resistor" refers to anyone who in a given situation has persistently resisted a change. The word is used throughout this book as a literary convenience, not as a means of labeling the whole person. Some of us are resistors a lot of the time; some of us are seldom resistors. A person who resists one kind of change may welcome another.

Joan is a long-time, trusted employee. You have few problems with her performance, except in her repeated refusals to be more positive and outgoing in her dealings with customers. Once again you ask her to be more upbeat with customers, and her defense is that her personality and style is more quiet and reserved. That's just the way she is, she says, and she can't change.

When Joan and employees like her are resisting, they often use psychology as a way of justifying their behavior. They are ever so happy to remind us that it is nearly impossible for them to change because of the way they were raised, or because of their psychological makeup. When they are asked to make a change, they simply point to the prevailing psychology and quote it.

"Well, you know me. I've done it this way forever. You can't teach an old dog new tricks."

"I can't do that. I've never been able to talk in front of people. I'm just too insecure to get up in front of all those people. You can't expect me to deliver that report."

"You want me to do what? Account for every nickel? I'm just not that detail-oriented. You'll have to get one of those bean counters to do it. It's more their thing."

People use these explanations to justify their resistance and avoid making changes. Resistors win with this limiting psychological analysis. And, occasionally, we use it ourselves to absolve ourselves of responsibility.

"Look, I'm sorry my department isn't following procedure on that, but what did you expect? I've got a bunch of independent entrepreneurial types down there, and no one can convince that group of renegades to sit in the office and fill out those reports."

Most of the time, however, we cannot afford this failure to perform, no matter how exotic the justification. We have to come up with results, not rationalizations. Faced with real, practical problems, we need an approach that provides workable solutions. If popular psychology isn't getting the job done, it's time to consider abandoning these traditional explanations and assumptions in favor of a more constructive alternative.

Breaking Through the Boundaries of Tradition

Meet Lauren. Everyone who knows her would say she has a strong need for attention. She's driving along the highway at a comfortable 75–80 miles per hour, when out on the horizon she spots a black and white police car idling under the overpass. Given her strong need for attention, does she turn on her lights to attract the patrol car? Like most of us, she probably lifts her foot off the gas, starts tapping the brakes, and eases into the slow lane in an attempt to avoid the attention of the officer in the patrol car. A psychological need for attention has nothing to do with Lauren's behavior. The consequences of being noticed in this situation are likely to be bad—a hefty fine and higher insurance rates—so she behaves accordingly.

Having successfully avoided the patrol car, Lauren drives another two miles when suddenly her car starts wheezing asthmatically. She steers onto the shoulder, feeling defeated. A glance in the rearview mirror reveals that coming up rapidly behind her is that same patrol car. Now, she jumps out of her car and waves frantically. Is Lauren seeking the officer's attention because of the sudden salience of her need for attention? We know the dramatic change in behavior has nothing to do with some latent psychological need. The consequences of attracting this officer's attention now seem positive—an immediate call to a tow truck and help with her car—and it's the likelihood that those consequences will occur that produce the change in her behavior.

You're on an airplane bound for yet another meeting. Once again, the flight attendant is on the microphone explaining emergency procedures and demonstrating safety equipment. You've heard this speech so many times you could give it yourself, complete with visual aids and hand gestures. You pay little attention, checking your watch, gazing out the window, flipping through the in-flight magazine.

Safety analysts say that your negative attitude toward safety and feelings of boredom cause your inattention. This fits neatly with a psychological analysis that says attitudes and feelings cause behavior.

Halfway through the flight, the flight attendant is back on the microphone. This time, she prefaces her emergency instructions by telling you that the plane is experiencing mechanical difficulties. The pilot will be making an emergency landing in Columbia, Missouri. Now you're all eyes and ears. You listen to every word and follow every gesture closely. You look up to identify the compartment containing your oxygen mask, and crane your neck to see the emergency exit doors. You vie with fellow passengers to get your questions answered.

These sudden changes in behavior are difficult to neatly explain using popular psychology, which assumes that change is rare because the underlying causes of behavior are buried in the past. In fact, we see that people act differently when the consequences in the *present* situation change. Consider the implications of this reality. If the cause of behavior is in the present, it's directly accessible to us. We don't have to spend months, or years, sifting through childhood experiences to discover why people act as they do, and to change that behavior.

As more and more women entered the American workforce in the 1970s, management analysts and women's advocates began to ask why more women weren't represented in the upper echelons of American business. Psychologists studied the question and determined that women were held back by their personality characteristics. According to the analysis, most men develop a fear of failure and a desire for success at an early age. These two forces prompt men to strive for high achievement and to always want to win.

Women were said to acquire the same fear of failure and desire for success, but these were frequently joined to a fear of success. As many as two-thirds of young women were said to suffer from an inner conflict between wanting to succeed and simultaneously fearing that success. This approach-avoidance conflict resulted in anxiety, and the high anxiety, in turn, interfered with job performance. Poor job performance interferes with promotions. And that, the psychologists concluded, is why more women don't have corner offices in the upper suites.

As with most such psychological analyses, women's lower level of achievement was blamed on their past experiences. When these women were young, they were told that boys wouldn't like them if they beat them at their own games. Worse, if the boys didn't like them, they wouldn't marry, wouldn't have children, and they would end their lives as old maids, societal failures. (Another version of this kind of theorizing asserted that because women hadn't played team sports, or been in the military, they'd never compete effectively.) While it's true that many women were sent these messages, that doesn't necessarily mean those messages caused the problem.

Fortunately for over half of the population, there is a more realistic explanation of why many talented women don't make it into the upper echelons. Researchers at the University of Southern California devised a series of studies to compare the popular psychological interpretations with an analysis emphasizing the role of consequences in shaping behavior. A group of women, all having been identified as having a fear of success, were asked to participate in a study in which they would be in competition with several men.

Some of the women were taken aside prior to the study and told privately to assume that their performance was going to be observed by a corporate recruiter. If they turned in **high**-level performances, they would be considered for extremely attractive, high-paying positions. The other women participating in the study were told that the recruiter would be looking for people who performed at an **average** level. *These* individuals would be selected for the attractive, high-paying jobs. To make this anomalous situation plausible, these women were told that through experience the company had learned that high performers usually turned out to be troublesome prima donnas, so the company decided to just hire good solid, average people.

Since both groups had the same personality disposition to fear success, only the consequences of their
behavior were different in the two situations. According to the psychological theory of fear of success, all of
the women should have performed at an average level
because all had the same enduring personality characteristic. If they were all fearful of success, they should
all have experienced anxiety and their performance
should have suffered. What, then, were the findings?

Women told that moderate performance would be
rewarded with positive consequences did indeed turn
in moderate performances. This could be due to the
favorable consequences in that situation, or it could be
an indication that an enduring fear of success does in
fact consistently cripple the performance of these
women.

The critical finding was in the achievement of the
women who were told that high performance would
win big rewards. The fear of success notion would
predict moderate performance here because of their
enduring personality characteristic. Far from being
crippled by a personality characteristic, however, these
women performed at exceptionally high levels. The
level of achievement of the two comparable groups of
women differed dramatically in the two situations because the consequences were different.

Similar studies were conducted with men. You remember them, the gender that supposedly always
wants to succeed. They too, were divided into groups
and told the same stories. Did the men always turn in
top performances? Hardly.

The men who thought they would be rewarded for
high performance performed highly. But, the men told
they would be rewarded for moderate performance
performed moderately. The men reacted just as the

women did in the two situations. They tailored their output to the rewarding consequences in the particular situation.

While these studies were carried out under laboratory conditions, in real life there are many work situations where the immediate consequences of high performance are in fact negative. Do really good work, and what happens?

You are hard-working and talented, and you have always been willing to take on added duties. In the year and a half you have been with the firm, your manager has learned he can count on you in a crisis.

"Look, I know this is a lot to ask, but you're the only one here I can trust with something this complicated."

You get more work, harder work, and you get to do it in your free time!

"Nobody else is capable of handling this and it absolutely has to be in Washington by Tuesday. Could you get it done this weekend?"

Even if your manager doesn't punish you for your high performance, your co-workers probably will.

"Thanks a lot. Now Clark is going to expect all of us to work on weekends when he's got some special project going."

Some supervisors inadvertently teach their employees that it doesn't pay to do too much. If employees continue to receive the same rewards regardless of how well they perform, but the high performers get more and more costly and time-consuming work, then moderate performance yields the better cost-benefit ratio. It's an equation that practically guarantees mediocrity.

Think about your own behavior. Examine it honestly, and you'll probably find that you too play dumb and hide your true capabilities when it pays. Have you ever made a remark such as the following:

"I don't know how to refill the paper for the copier. Can you help me, Irene?"

"I'd be happy to take the minutes of the meeting, but my handwriting is practically illegible. Better ask someone else."

"You know, Terry, you're much better at details than I am. Why don't I begin with a few general remarks to set the context, then you can do the detailed part of the presentation?"

Have you been in a meeting and stifled the urge to make a suggestion because you knew the leader would immediately assign you the responsibility for implementing the idea?

It's the reward system in the workplace that dictates the level of performance, not an employee's personality or his past. People can switch from top output to mediocrity according to the consequences of their actions. If someone resists your request for change, don't blame it on their attitude, their need for control, or their lack of confidence. Ask yourself how it might benefit this person to object to your request, and you will see that people resist change when it produces *more* negative consequences—more work, more supervision, less advancement opportunity—than positive consequences. When there are more benefits than costs, people welcome change.

As president of a software company providing products for the resort industry, you believe there is a place for everyone, but you haven't found the right one for Clint. You inherited him when you bought the company, and he always has a negative word for everyone else's work. Fortunately he is only three years from retirement, but unfortunately every project he touches turns sour. So far he has vigorously resisted your attempts to reassign him away from programming, but you make one more try.

The new job as customer liaison and troubleshooter doesn't demand much work, but it does require several midwinter trips to Hawaii. It also carries an impressive title, a salary hike, and an expense account. Because Clint will be gone for extended periods of time, he will also be allowed to take his significant other with him on the Hawaii trips at company expense.

You are surprised when Clint asserts that he does not want a job that requires frequent trips to Hawaii. He tells you that he is sensitive to heat, and besides, his wife lived in Hawaii in the past and left for good reasons. Clint resists this change, because for him the negative consequences outweigh the benefits of the assignment. When you suggest a job in the quality control department, which doesn't involve any travel, he accepts with pleasure.

While this example suggests that change *can* happen quickly, that doesn't mean that it always does. In many situations, people not only appear to behave in consistent patterns, they do behave consistently. The question is why? One answer would be to attribute this consistency to their enduring psychological characteristics. The other interpretation suggests that they keep behaving in the same patterns because the consequences of their actions remain the same.

You manage a retail outlet and Vivien is a talented but troublesome sales clerk. She is exceptionally good with customers, but she is very sensitive to criticism. No matter what you say, or how constructively you try to say it, Vivien takes it very personally. The least hint of criticism prompts sulking, withdrawal, or tears.

Perhaps this sensitivity is caused by her excessive need for approval, or by her feelings of insecurity and her low self-esteem. See what you discover when you look only at the consequences of Vivien's "sensitivity."

Through her repeated displays of tears and silent sulking, Vivien has "trained" you not to criticize her. Every time you suggest that she assume a greater share of the collective workload, you have to spend the next hour tending to her hurt feelings instead of the store. To avoid these emotional scenes, you treat her with kid gloves.

Since you don't criticize her, Vivien is free to do things her way. As you might guess, Vivien's way is the one which doesn't involve any of the drudgery of day-to-day operations. She merrily chats with customers, even after they have made their purchases, while you and the other clerks stock the shelves, check inventory, and tag new merchandise.

You, and most everyone else, have made it pay for Vivien to "be" sensitive. By consistently yielding to her hypersensitive manner, the people around her enable her to consistently do the easy parts of the job, and to avoid its negative aspects. In Vivien's world, it almost always pays for her to be sensitive.

Even the most consistent behavior can change, however, when the consequences change. Consider Tony, who is a top sales person for a firm that manufactures large business signs. Tony is a big shot, and he gets away with murder. He's loud, he's opinionated, and everybody knows it's Tony's way or nothing.

Popular psychology tells us that Tony's abrasive manner is due to his overinflated ego. Or, it might be that he is trying to hide his insecurity. Either way, the implication is that Tony constantly acts like a prima donna.

What happens when we examine Tony's antics for their consequences? We find that people react to his tantrums and bullyboy tactics by doing things the way he wants just so they can keep him quiet. Thus, the agenda of the luncheon meeting is rearranged so Tony can leave early. Everybody agrees to hold the meeting at the Italian place because that's Tony's favorite. And once there, it is only natural for Tony to be served first. Remember he has to leave early.

Until now it has consistently paid for Tony to act like a prima donna. But times change and Tony goes into a sales slump, which lasts for months. At the end of the third quarter, Tony, once the top dog, is now low man on the totem pole. Slowly but surely, reactions to his bullying tactics begin to change. The regional sales manager no longer gives in to him. Instead of letting Tony's behavior continue unchecked, he tells Tony in no uncertain terms that he'd better stop talking and start producing, or he'll find himself out on the street. If Tony can't find another job in a hurry, he'll probably change his style pretty fast. His loud opinions are likely to become deferential suggestions. A new set of consequences could transform this prima donna into a team player.

Look at how many people consistently refuse to work Saturdays when it's straight pay, but will suddenly be free when it's double time. Watch how quickly people can learn the new computer system when the top five operators will be given bonus prizes, and how slowly they learn when it will simply earn them extra work. Producing change, and solving people problems, is an interpersonal process in which you alter the consequences of the other person's actions, so that it is more beneficial for them to do what you want than to do the opposite.

A MORE OPTIMISTIC APPROACH

Two words, behavior and consequences, are the essence of this fresh approach to people and problems. Instead of attempting to analyze people, analyze the way specific, observable consequences affect their behavior. Instead of trying to change psychic entities buried in people's heads, change the consequences of their actions.

This alternative approach goes beyond traditional psychological explanations. It doesn't deny that people have thoughts and feelings. Instead of using these psychological processes as explanations, however, it goes on to identify the real-world consequences that make people think and feel the way they do.

Switching from a language of broad psychological labels to specific behaviors and consequences also involves a change of time reference. Rather than looking back into a person's past, look to the consequences in the here and now.

People who are trying to resist change will use the past as a way of justifying why they can't act differently. It serves their self-interest to lure you into a long discussion of how their past personal and cultural experiences make it impossible for them to change. However, you don't have to learn the traumatic details of someone's past history to effectively deal with them in the workplace. Change is no longer dependent on your capacity to understand a person's deep psychological makeup and how he got that way. Change is dependent only on your ability to structure consequences in present and future situations.

Practically speaking, the past is irrelevant to change, but that doesn't mean that nothing was learned, or acquired, in the past. We all learned a very great deal in the past. We learned how to cooperate and how to compete. We learned how to act selfishly and how to play as part of a team. We learned how to meet deadlines and how to miss them. We learned how to be responsible and how to be irresponsible. We learned how to be productive and counterproductive.

On the job there are, of course, technical skills that require specialized training. But for your garden-variety people problem, you can safely assume that people already know how to do what you want them to do. The procrastinator you are lecturing this afternoon on the importance of meeting deadlines probably gave his sleepy-eyed daughter the same lecture only this morning. The person unable to grasp your request that she start sharing her reports for the good of the department just finished telling her children to share their toys. The man unable to learn the new participative management techniques because he's too old a dog to learn new tricks is the same one who practices consensus-building at his club meetings every Tuesday.

Each of these people has learned at some time in the past all of the behaviors you want them to perform, but people play dumb, hoping you won't keep asking them to change. If you continue to blame your workplace problems on things outside your control—other people's attitudes, values, beliefs, personalities, needs, emotions, or self-esteem—you may actually be facilitating their resistance. If you shift your focus to the consequences that produce the problem behavior, you can stop people from behaving in nonproductive ways.

This new interpretation implies that you are responsible for your problem cases. Your familiar escape routes of labeling and blaming the person are no longer available, and you are no longer absolved from responsibility if you try but are unable to solve the problem. This can be more than a little daunting.

Take a second look, however, and you'll find the new approach liberating. It offers you a way to fix your people problems, not just a way to fix the blame. Since you are the one arranging the consequences that cause the problem behaviors, you have a large measure of control over the solution. You can change the way you are dealing with other people and how they are dealing with you. You can make your work relationships more productive, more versatile, and more agreeable, and you can begin to act in the ways you've always wanted, to achieve all the things you hoped to achieve.

Until now, most of us have been trapped by the limits of the traditional analysis of people problems. Convinced that we couldn't change people, we were therefore convinced that we couldn't solve people problems. Believing in the impossibility of change, we were too quick to give in and make it pay for people to resist change.

With this new approach to analyzing and solving people problems, you will see that change is clearly possible, and that it is easily within your ability to produce it. This practical approach frees you from the burdens of the past. It unchains you from the idea that change is an onerous, difficult task instead of a relatively common and uncomplicated process. Most freeing of all, this new analysis clearly shows that none of us are fixed one way or stuck forever in rigid patterns of behavior.

The tools you need for managing change and for overcoming resistance can be learned easily and practiced immediately. With this new approach, change becomes not only possible but positively inviting.

C H A P T E R   T W O

Getting Down to Ground Level

In reading the following pairs of statements, see how quickly you can pick the one statement in each pair most likely to produce change.

A. "Be more customer-oriented."
B. "No phone should ring more than three times."

A. "Be more positive and friendly."
B. "I want you to smile and say, 'How may I help you?' to the next ten customers who come through the door."

A. "We have to improve quality."
B. "The reject rate must be below 1.5 percent by the end of the month."

A. "Bring in more new customers."
B. "By the end of the day, I want you to give me the names of five new potential clients, along with their phone numbers, addresses, and the purchasing agent."

In each pair, statement B is more specific, concrete, and more likely to prompt someone to change immediately. Yet that's not how we usually ask for change. Time and again, we make the broad, sweeping requests seen in the A statements, requests that in fact accomplish nothing.

We make these broad requests when we try to solve our people problems because we tend to use broad terms to define our people problems. That's our biggest stumbling block. The way we describe our problems shapes the way we attempt to solve them.

Listen to the words people use when talking about people problems in the workplace. Draw up a list of The Top Ten Office People Problems and see if it includes these phrases:

> He's such a prima donna.
> She's too sensitive.
> He can't see the big picture.
> She's too emotional.
> He's a steamroller.
> She's not a team player.
> He procrastinates.
> She's completely self-centered.
> He lacks initiative.
> She's not committed.
> He's not assertive enough.

Everybody uses these terms. They sound familiar and their familiarity makes them sound true. But if you switch from thinking about the problem to thinking about its solution, you will see why these descriptions are useless.

Such generalities fail to specify exactly what the other person is supposed to change. Instead, they make the people problems seem huge and unsolvable and, confronted by these gigantic, seemingly intractable cases, we give up on them. Furthermore, these lofty pronouncements have disastrous effects on future communication. You probably see this on a daily basis at work or at home.

Consider Nick, one of your product managers. Nick has trouble delegating work, and when he does delegate, he ends up redoing all of the work other people have done. One day you confront him about his management style, telling him that he is overly controlling. How does Nick react to this pronouncement? He'll probably flare out in anger, self-righteously deny the accusation, or start blaming other people. It makes little difference which of these responses he chooses. They all produce the same result.

What should have been a simple request turns into a gigantic emotional confrontation. Communication breaks down completely. You storm away, dead certain that it's absolutely no use trying to talk to the man. He storms off in the opposite direction, convinced that you're a tyrant.

In the future, Nick will use your global indictments to create an emotional smokescreen that diverts you from your request for change. He'll deny your charges and before long you'll be concentrating on the argument instead of on the change. This diversion enables

Nick to successfully avoid change for the time being. And when you get so upset that you quit talking to him altogether, you will have helped him even more. Now, he's also successfully avoided change for the future.

Talking about people problems in broad terms and trying to solve those problems with requests that are just as broad is about as effective as trying to zap that nasty patch of dandelions in your lawn from the window of an airliner as you're flying overhead. You're too far away from the problem to do anything about it.

USING YOUR ALTIMETER

Think back to the last time you flew in a jet airliner. At the standard cruising altitude of 30,000 to 40,000 feet, you're most likely to see just cloud cover. When there is a break in the clouds, you can make out only major land masses and large bodies of water. As the plane descends for landing and you reach about 20,000 feet, you break through the clouds. Now you can see that you're approaching the airport and that it's still about 50 miles distant. Descending to 10,000 feet, you can now clearly distinguish truck and automobile traffic on highways and streets. As you approach ground level for touchdown, you're once more at eye level with the details of daily life clearly in view.

To get a clear picture of exactly what is going on, you have to get out of the clouds and down to earth. To solve people problems, you must do precisely the same thing. You have to quit thinking and talking in 40,000-foot generalities, and begin thinking and talking at ground level.

We'll soon discuss techniques that can be used to bring any problem people down out of the stratosphere, but let's first examine the major altitude levels we'll have to get through to land safely and start producing change.

40,000 Feet and Climbing. You know you are heading for the ionosphere when you hear people using labels such as lazy, unprofessional, incompetent, paranoid, argumentative, rigid, two-faced, old-fashioned, or defensive. These labels are little more than indictments of the other person's character or ability. They convey much more anger than meaning, so they result in more hostility than change.

30,000 Feet. This is the psychological level. Problems are defined here in terms of thoughts and feelings. We say someone doesn't care, understand, or listen. They lack initiative, commitment, and enthusiasm. She should be more logical, assertive, creative, and thoughtful. He should be less negative, emotional, and narrow-minded.

These descriptions may sound more precise, but really they have very little meaning. They focus on what the person is assumed to think, or feel, but not on what they are supposed to do. As a result, little gets done.

These words give resistors another escape route. If you've talked about attitudes, values, and beliefs, or emotions, the resistor could now turn about-face and completely agree with you. He'll say you've made him see things in an entirely new light. Thanks to you, he's adopted a new attitude, has a whole new outlook, or feels entirely different about the subject at hand.

Unfortunately, this is only pseudo-agreement. He'll keep acting the same old way he always has. His new state of mind produces no change in behavior. If you want action, you'll have to get to ground level.

20,000 Feet. At this level, patterns become clear.

We begin to define the problem in terms of actions and outcomes, but the terms are still very general. We talk about the need to improve sales, provide better service, be more communicative, bring in more customers, and reduce errors. While such descriptions do at least imply action, the actions are not stated explicitly.

To appreciate the ambiguity of these statements, imagine doing a completely new job. You go to work for an entirely new company, in a different industry, on a job for which you have no training and little experience. At the beginning of the first day, you are handed a sheaf of personnel forms and, after brief introductions to fellow employees, your supervisor tells you that your job is to bring in new customers for the company's frozen food line.

You're bound to have an entire list of questions. "What are the products in the frozen food line?" "Who are our existing customers?" "Is there a specific territory I'm supposed to work for new customers?" "How many new customers and how fast?" From your supervisor's briefing, you still don't know exactly what you are supposed to do. The descriptions at this 20,000 foot level still aren't specific enough.

10,000 Feet. At 10,000 feet, actions come into focus. The recommendation that Jane "take more initiative" now means that she suggest new applications and new markets for our existing product lines. "Provide better service" is stated as "answer the phone promptly." "Improve sales" is translated into "spend more time on the phone with customers and less time in the employees' lounge." The problem is being discussed in more concrete behavioral terms.

Defining what you want in terms of action makes your request clear, and makes it more difficult for the resistor to avoid doing it. In many situations, these 10,000-foot descriptions may be sufficiently detailed definitions of what you want. Some people, however, are virtual professionals at resisting change and, to handle their tactics, you have to get to absolute ground level.

Ground Level. This is reality. Down here, you are describing exactly what actions you want the other person to perform. "Spend more time on the phone" is stated as "make at least fifteen customer calls per day, and no personal calls." "Suggest new ideas" translates to "At the beginning of each month's planning meeting, I want every manager to describe two new product applications and one new market for our existing products." You know you are at ground level if you can state the problem in terms of quantifiable actions and outcomes.

At first, you may have some reservations about spelling things out at ground level. You may realize that you'll get only the actions that you specifically ask for, and yet you want a lot more. But, after you get one thing you want, then you can go after another, and another, and another. It may take a little more time, but in the long run you'll see that it is much more efficient to proceed one change at a time than to try to change everything at once.

You may also be uneasy about using this ground-level approach because you're picturing the wrong audience. If you imagine yourself being this specific with a valued employee who almost always does what you want him to do, who anticipates necessary actions and suggests them, and who adapts to changing circumstances, your unease is justified.

Although clear communication may benefit you

both, you won't have to get down to such specifics with good employees. However, if an employee who usually fulfills your requests quickly fails to do what you ask, your request may have been too general. Bring it down to ground level so that he knows exactly what you want.

Specifying exactly what you want may be frustrating because you believe that the person already knows what it is you want him to do. You are probably right, but a person resisting change is not likely to admit it. Instead, he will feign ignorance as a way to avoid change. Don't let him get away with it. Take a little added time and politely state your request in extremely precise terms.

Ground-level definitions are essential when it comes to making changes in the actions of employees who have repeatedly resisted your requests. With such hard-core resistors, you must be able to state precisely what you want them to do. If you get even a few feet above the ground—allowing any room for interpretation—they'll slip away from you, and you may not get another chance.

Angelica has been appointed head of the athletic ticket office at a major university. By tradition this has been a "man's" job, but she has taken a slipshod operation and made it run very smoothly. She has been successful with most of the existing staff, except for Ned, who is consistently tardy. In an effort to get him to be on time, she avoids such words as irresponsible, bad attitude, poor work habits, or even saying the guy is coming to work late. Instead, she strives for zero altitude by telling him, "I want you to be at work by eight o'clock."

The next day Angelica purposely walks by Ned's

office at 8:01 to see if he's there. As has become his habit, he's nowhere to be seen. She attends to some pressing matters back at her office and then returns to check on Ned a half hour later. He's at his desk, and he's all smiles.

"Why weren't you here at eight o'clock?" Angelica asks.

Naturally, Ned says, "I was here." But Ned's definition of here is broader than Angelica's. "I was in the parking lot," he explains.

Realizing that she didn't get specific enough, Angelica tries again. "Tomorrow, I want you at your desk by eight o'clock."

This is better, but it may not be good enough. When she checks the next day, she may find Ned at his desk, but his desk will be covered with the morning's newspaper and one of his buddies will be there talking about the sports page.

Distasteful and juvenile as it may seem, with the really tough cases, you may have to spell out the behavior you want in agonizing detail. For Angelica, it means telling Ned, "Tomorrow, I want you at your desk and working by eight o'clock. In other words, no newspaper, no coffee cups, no friends around, and no radio. Just you and your computer, up and running."

When dealing with people who have resisted change over and over again, the first critical skill is developing the ability to precisely state the exact actions you want performed. The many techniques and tools to be described later in this book depend on using ground-level definitions.

DEFINING YOUR TERMS

Most of us have difficulty stating the exact actions we want from another person. When pressed to get down to earth, we end up in a holding pattern at the high altitudes, using one ambiguous synonym after another. "I want you to be more enthusiastic," you might say to your department manager. "Show some energy. You know, be more positive. Don't be so negative. Be more optimistic instead of so pessimistic. Understand?" He probably doesn't.

As you work on defining some of your own people problems, you will probably find yourself stuck at the higher elevations. While it may seem challenging at first, with practice you'll be able to refine your change requests until you automatically lay down your terms at ground level.

Try this as an exercise. Take out a piece of paper—please don't do this in your head—and write the name and the problem of your target person at the top of the page. Then write one or two phrases that describe the problem. Keep rewriting the problem in increasingly specific action language.

Begin with a typical 40,000-foot indictment. The sales department is lazy. They had it easy in good times when all they had to do was sit back and write orders. Now, when times are tough, they don't want to get out and do any work.

Asking the right questions will help you focus your complaint. To get down from 40,000 feet, the basic question to ask yourself is: *What do you want the sales people to* **do**? Suppose your answer to this is that you would like them to care more and be more energized.

Now you have defined the problem at the 30,000-foot psychological level as a matter of feelings.

Next, try a slightly different question and see if it gets you down closer to reality: *How would the salespeople act if they weren't lazy?* They would make more sales calls. Congratulations! Now you've dropped down to talking about broad patterns of outcomes and actions at about 20,000 feet.

To drop lower, focus on behavior in a specific situation or a particular part of their job responsibilities. *To whom should they be making more sales calls?* Rather than selling to new customers, the sales department should be concentrating on selling more product lines to our existing customers. That's even more precise. You've now brought your request down to 10,000 feet by emphasizing one part of their activities.

To get to ground level, hunt for the ambiguous words in your previous definition. For example, what do you mean by "selling more product lines"? *What exact actions do you want the salespeople to take and how do you want them to do it?* Spell out the specific actions you want. Your final request might sound something like this:

"When you call on each of your regular customers, take an extra five minutes and show them at least three of our products that they are not currently purchasing. Ask if they'd like to order any of these three. If they decline, ask what we could do to make the products attractive enough for them to buy. Write down their answers and give them to me with your orders by 5 o'clock on Friday."

Good Questions and Bad Questions

Try one more. You have someone who's not a team player. You ask yourself what the problem is and decide that he thinks only about himself. This puts you at the psychological level, talking in terms of his thoughts and feelings.

Many of us are very tempted to ask why. Why is this person this way? Do not ask why. Asking why usually only yields psychological dead-end answers such as "he's narcissistic." "He thinks he's better than everyone." "He was the baby in his family and everything was given to him so he has a big ego." This puts you into a holding pattern at the 30,000-foot level of personalities, thoughts, and egos, and does nothing to help you solve the problem.

Stay out of the person's past, and stay out of his head. Focus instead on the present and on what you want the person to do or stop doing. Your answer may be that you want him to cooperate more with his co-workers. This sounds good, familiar, and true, but it is still too general.

If you're stuck up in the clouds, try a new question that may break the holding pattern: *how would a top-performing employee act in this situation?* If your answer is that he would be more considerate toward his co-workers, you are still at the psychological level of "thoughts."

Return to the earlier approach of thinking about specific parts of the person's job, or specific times and situations when his behavior causes the most trouble. Now you might realize that his behavior is most counterproductive during times of peak production and right before delivery deadlines.

Focusing only on this situation, rephrase the basic question in terms of how you want him to act in these circumstances. If you say that you want him to assist his co-workers when work backs up during peak production, you are getting lower but there are still 10,000 feet to ground level. Can you identify any ambiguous words in that definition? What do you mean by "assist"?

Write down exactly what you mean by "assist." "When you finish your own work, go to your co-workers and ask if they have any work with which you can help. Ask this in a civil tone of voice and tell them you will be happy to help them finish their assignment." Spell it out in precise ground-level terms.

Another universal complaint is that someone lacks people skills. While everyone may nod their heads as if they know what you mean when you say this, you are actually talking up at the 40,000-foot level.

The managing partner of a law firm complains that new law school graduates know the law, but they don't know how to be lawyers. Her conception of the problem is that these new hires don't know how to deal with people.

Let's find out what the specific problem is. When asked, the managing partner said that the recent grads weren't tough-minded. She quickly added that this was because they lacked self-confidence. This sounds plausible, and it also sounds as though we're answering the "why" question in psychological terms up at 30,000 feet.

Using the technique of imagining how an ideal attorney would act enabled her to focus on a positive example and to get down a little lower. "Compared to more seasoned attorneys, the new hires are poor negotiators." So, it is how they negotiate that she is interested in. That's an improvement, but she was still talking about a fairly wide range of behavior at the 20,000-foot level.

When asked what specific negotiation skills she wanted, she answered, "You know—negotiate better. Get better deals." Since that question didn't yield results, she was asked to identify a particular situation in which it was important that the new attorneys become better negotiators. "It's most important that they negotiate better in their initial telephone conversations with opposing counsel. They give in to any request from the other side, folding like a bunch of paper dolls."

By identifying the situations in which the problem arose, she was able to move down to the 10,000-foot level, focusing on the new lawyers' "giving in" patterns. As you may already have determined, "giving in" is still not very precise. When asked, "How would they act, if they were not giving in easily?" her response was quick and to the point. "When an opposing counsel asked for a continuance, they'd say let me think about it instead of automatically agreeing. They'd hang up the phone and make up a list of things they wanted. Then they could call back and propose a compromise in which the opposing counsel would give us something in return for our agreeing to his request." Now she is describing the actual things she wants her new attorneys to say and do. Touchdown!

At ground level, the first change the new attorneys made was to start making lists of specific things they wanted from the opposing counsel prior to any phone conversation. Endless speeches and pep talks about being more confident and assertive did little good, but defining exactly what she wanted the lawyers to do produced measurable results.

COMMON PROBLEMS IN THE WORKPLACE

In the following cases, some common problems are defined at 40,000 feet, then 30, 20, 10, and finally ground level. This is to give you a better sense of the process of refining your definition, and is not meant to suggest that every time you analyze a problem you must work through each successive level. If you can go straight from 40K to touchdown, that is ideal. In fact, as you develop your skill at defining problems, that ground level touchdown will come quickly.

Some of the characters in these case studies may remind you of people you have to deal with at work. You may want to use pen and paper to work on your own ground-level definitions. If you do, bear in mind these basic questions:

What do I want him to do?
How would he act if he were a top performer?
In what situations is this problem most troubling to me?
Exactly what actions do I want him to perform?
How, when, where, and with whom do I want him to do it?
How much, or how many times, do I want him to do it and by what time deadline?

As you go through this process, you may discover that there are many specific things you want the person to do. It helps to write them all down and then take them on, one change at a time.

Procrastination. We all know procrastinators, and in some instances may be guilty ourselves. Consider Stan, who's head of production at a manufacturing facility. Stan is consistently late with his schedules, but labeling him as a procrastinator is a useless 40,000-foot indictment, and saying that his problem is a lack of foresight and problem anticipation doesn't suggest a solution, either.

Saying that Stan should do more planning is still too broad a definition of the desired actions. More specific still is the statement that Stan should work out the production schedules in advance. Down at ground level, the problem is finally defined. "By the 25th, I want you to give me the list of the completion dates for each of next month's projects. List the possible problems that might arise on each project and how they will be handled." That's it: concrete actions.

No Follow-through. A manager complained that his people were good at saying they would do something, but not very good at following through on their promises. When asked what specific things people weren't following through on, this manager complained that his supervisors didn't care about safety.

Upon further questioning, he said that his supervisors wouldn't talk with their people about safety. The word "talk" is very ambiguous and clearly he wanted more than just any old talk. The manager became more animated as he thought specifically about what kind of talk he wanted and when he wanted it. He explained that he wanted the supervisors to hold a safety meeting once a month.

He got down to ground level when he began itemizing the exact topics he wanted discussed. He wanted the managers to tell their subordinates how to use safety equipment, how to handle toxic substances, and what the appropriate first-aid procedures were in specific situations. He also wanted the supervisors to ask the crews for specific ideas about how safety could be improved. Armed with this list of concrete behaviors, he was much more successful in getting his supervisors to do exactly what he wanted.

Did you have any idea of what he had in mind when he said he wanted more follow-through? Even knowing that he was talking about matters of safety didn't enable us to know the specific changes he wanted to make in his staff's behavior. Just as you couldn't tell what this manager had in mind, people have great difficulty knowing what you mean when you use high-altitude descriptions.

Insensitivity. How many bosses across the world each day counsel a supervisor to be more sensitive to other people? And how much good do these counseling sessions do? Usually none.

Telling a person he is insensitive usually produces defensiveness and bad feelings, but doesn't change behavior. You haven't told the person how you want him to behave. Telling him to listen and pay attention to people is a description of what should go on in his head but not what he should do. Advising the person not to "act so defensively when customers are making complaints" specifies the setting in which you desire action, but it doesn't precisely indicate what actions you want.

A ground-zero request might sound like this. "Smile and nod your head when a customer is talking. Don't interrupt a customer who is making a complaint. Ask the customer what he would like you to do about the problem. Get the customer's phone number and tell him you will contact him within forty-eight hours with your manager's decision on the matter. And please, always thank the customer for giving us the opportunity to address his concern.''

Chauvinism. Here's another label that carries more emotion than meaning. In casual conversation, it may be convenient to define the problem person as a chauvinist, but that isn't specific enough if you are going to produce change. Saying the guy is prejudiced and that he's covering his own feelings of inferiority is too psychological.

Where and how does this chauvinism manifest itself? "In meetings, this jerk makes disrespectful remarks about women." What does he say or do that is disrespectful? "He's always sarcastic and takes cuts at women's interests and abilities." What do you want him to do at the next meeting? "I don't want him to say 'Well, what do the ladies think? They always have an opinion.' ''

Start by getting him to stop making these particular remarks. No doubt there are additional remarks you also want to squelch, and you can take them on one at a time down at this concrete level. Then, start working on the specific kinds of remarks that you want him to make.

Unprofessional Behavior. Sharon, your midwestern regional sales manager, is not always as professional as you would like her to be. There are countless ways in which a person can be unprofessional, and until you define the problem at ground level, it isn't clear what exact changes you want Sharon to make.

At the 30,000-foot psychological level, Sharon's lack of professionalism might be viewed as a lack of principles or values. Because she lacks these values, what does she do, or fail to do? The response to this question might be that she has poor communication habits.

Getting still more precise, it was Sharon's habit of using offensive language that was the problem. This was especially problematic when she was conducting her regional sales meetings, so it was the elimination of profanity during meetings that the national sales director wanted changed in this instance. Who would have ever guessed that was the real issue when the original description was that Sharon was unprofessional?

Low Productivity. A retailer complained that her sales people were unproductive. She explained that what she meant was that they weren't enthusiastic. As she tried to say exactly how this lack of enthusiasm was manifested, she emphasized that the clerks should do more with the displays. Clearly, "do more with the displays" is not very clear. She redefined her request, and said she wanted the clerks to check the displays regularly.

Now her request was nicely focused on behavior, but with some clerks she found she had to be even more explicit. She hit pay dirt by asking the clerks to check each display once every hour and fill in any missing items from inventory.

Lack of Initiative. A president couldn't understand his key managers' lack of initiative and would regularly regale them with speeches on the need for initiative. He'd cite his own past accomplishments at length. This produced dutiful nods of agreement but no action.

Privately, he said that his people just weren't creative types. Upon further analysis, he said that he wanted them to generate new ideas. In particular, he wanted ideas about the way paperwork was being handled.

At his next staff meeting, he announced that on the

first Monday of every month he wanted each department head to give him a written description of a new procedure being instituted to minimize paperwork (ground zero). At the next monthly meeting, he specified another change. He asked that managers also include a written evaluation of the effectiveness of each change three months after it was instituted.

Resistance to Change. Saying that someone is resistant to change is definitely up at 40,000 feet. The plant manager at a plastic injection molding company said he had a real tough case of resistance. Tom, an older engineer, was clinging to old ways of thinking out of fear. When the discussion moved away from the psychological cause and on to the specific old things to which Tom was clinging, the manager said that Tom refused to use the computer.

Now the problem came into focus. It became even sharper when the manager said that he wanted Tom to start using the CAD system for his drafting assignments. Finally, at ground level, the manager and Tom agreed upon the following concrete quantified behaviors: Tom agreed to practice on the CAD system once a day for fifteen uninterrupted minutes and every Friday he would bring in the drawings he'd made on the CAD system that week and spend thirty minutes reviewing what he'd learned with the manager.

Stating your requests in terms of specific behaviors, rather than ambiguous generalities, blocks resistors from using some of their favorite escape routes. When you talk up at the higher altitudes, the resistor can play dumb—acting as though he doesn't know what you mean. Another option is for the resistor to "misinterpret" what you meant. And you can bet that he'll interpret in such a way that he doesn't have to change. Or, the resistor may publicly promise to go along with your request, but that's all he'll do. He knows that your failure to be specific means you can't legitimately blame him for failing to do exactly what you wanted. After all, he'll retort, "You didn't tell me that was what you wanted me to do."

Using ground-level language is the single best thing you can do to improve your communications with others. When people know exactly what you mean, they are more likely to do it.

CHAPTER THREE

Trade Secrets

We rely on a restricted set of words and concepts to analyze our relationships.

"Dave and I **trust** each other."

"My boss doesn't **respect** me."

"Good **communication** is the key."

"I don't feel any **support** from her."

"We need more **cooperation** and **loyalty**."

Trust, respect, communication, support, and loyalty are commonly used but impractical general concepts. These descriptions are at too high an altitude to be useful in solving problems. They register at about 40,000 feet and miss most of the fine detail of what is really going on.

Using these general concepts to think about relationships creates the same oversimplifications that occur when we use global concepts and broad terms to analyze people problems. They leave too much room for misunderstanding, and they make it simple for resistors to avoid changing.

When you complain that you don't feel your boss is supporting you, he can easily resist by citing the one (and only) time in the last six months in which he publicly backed one of your requests. When you tell an employee that you want more cooperation, he can argue that he is cooperative, and he'll drag up a single instance to prove it. Just as it was necessary to move out of the clouds down to ground level to better understand people, we must become just as precise to understand relationships.

THE COSTS AND REWARDS OF RELATIONSHIPS

Relationships can be viewed as a process of exchange in which each party does specific things for and to the other person. The whole approach rests on the assumption that what counts in a relationship is what is observable, external, and measurable. The only thing that is generally observable and measurable is what people do. So the only thing that counts is behavior.

This may appear to be an innocuous statement, but it has startling implications. If only behavior counts, what doesn't count? All kinds of psychological things inside the person don't count—intentions, feelings, attitudes, etc. These internal phenomena, which are unobservable and unmeasurable, don't count until they are manifested in overt action.

The behaviors exchanged in relationships can be categorized as either costs or rewards. Behaviors the other person performs that have positive consequences for you are rewards. The greater the positive benefit to you, the greater their reward value for you. The other person's actions are costly for you if they result in negative consequences for you, and the more negative the consequences, the greater their costliness. The other person's actions can also be costly for him if they require time and energy that he could profitably spend in another relationship.

Rhett and Scarlett both work in the same real estate office, but in many ways they are worlds apart. Scarlett has been a star sales producer for several years, and Rhett passed his license exam only a few weeks ago. This is his first position. Despite these differences, the two exchange a number of behaviors each day.

When Rhett gets his first listing, Scarlett takes time to show him how to enter it into the multiple listing with the company's complicated software program. This is a reward to Rhett and a cost to Scarlett. During this encounter she discovers that Rhett is a computer whiz, and uses a laptop all the time. Since Scarlett is in the market for a laptop, she asks Rhett for some advice. That evening Rhett misses his weekly basketball game at the gym to stay late and demonstrate his laptop and give Scarlett some shopping tips. Now Rhett is incurring costs by forgoing his recreation, and Scarlett is receiving the rewarding benefits of his knowledge.

One day Rhett is at work very early and answers a call before the office officially opens. It's one of Scarlett's hot prospects calling from the airport prior to an international flight. Answering this call takes Rhett about two minutes, so it costs him very little. In placing three calls before finally locating her at the spa to give her the phone message, Rhett has given her another reward. And, it's a reward that can have different levels of value.

If a big sale with a nice commission attached results from Scarlett's prompt response to her client's call, then Rhett's quick action is a reward that's of considerable value. If the caller only wanted to convey that he was leaving the country for five days, Rhett's actions have much lower reward value for Scarlett.

As it turns out, because Rhett delivered the message promptly, Scarlett made the big sale. She spends the morning finalizing the purchase agreement and invites Rhett to a posh restaurant for lunch. After listening to Rhett talk about his frustrations as a new salesperson for over an hour, she spends two more hours giving him numerous pointers on how to succeed. The expensive lunch, plus Scarlett's patient listening and her hours of advice represent sizable costs to her and significant rewards to Rhett.

By the afternoon, the two have exchanged a number of behaviors, and it's possible to summarize the exchange to this point. We can approximate the reward and cost values on the behaviors exchanged in the relationship, and those approximations can serve as the baseline for our judgments about whether a relationship is good, bad, or terrible.

Good Relationships

A good relationship is both profitable and equitable for the people involved. If an individual's rewards are greater than his costs, the relationship is profitable for the person. Since the value of Rhett's rewards exceed the costs he is incurring, he is profiting. The rewards Scarlett has received thus far are greater than her costs, so she too is operating at a profit. That's half of what it takes to make a good relationship.

A relationship is equitable if the proportion of re-

wards to costs is the same for both people. When to-
taled, we might say Rhett's rewards are four times
greater than his costs. While Scarlett has received a
higher absolute amount of rewards than Rhett, her
costs have been correspondingly higher, so her overall
ratio is also four to one. Since the two proportions of
rewards to costs are equal, their relationship is equitable. The relationship is now both profitable and equitable and that means it's a good relationship.

Bad Relationships

Wednesday morning a newlywed couple shows up at
the real estate office, with Scarlett's card in hand. Scarlett is talking on the phone to another sales prospect,
and while covering the mouthpiece she asks Rhett to
entertain the newlyweds for a couple minutes, and
would he also be good enough to bring her a quick cup
of coffee (black with two NutraSweets). She's on the
phone for more than thirty minutes, while Rhett
wastes his valuable time listening to the newlyweds
complain about the price of housing. Rhett is incurring
costs and providing rewards to Scarlett.

Scarlett concludes the phone conversation and
takes over with the newlyweds. After she finds out they
can't qualify for a car loan, much less a house, she
guides them out the door with the promise to call them
when she finds their dream house. She then turns to
Rhett and asks if he would be a prince and go get the
key duplicated for one of her new listings. She tells him
this will be good experience, and to use her name with
the locksmith, so he can get a discount on this key and
his own in the future. Oh, and would he put the key in
the lockbox on the door of the new listing. With Rhett

serving as gofer, Scarlett is free to relax at the spa for the rest of the afternoon.

Rhett discovers the locksmith doesn't know Scarlett from Eve, and the new listing is away across town, not "right on his way home" as Scarlett claimed. At this point, the relationship is no longer equitable.

Scarlett has not been incurring any more costs, while her rewards have been climbing. Her overall ratio of rewards to costs is now approximately six to one. Rhett's rewards have only increased slightly, but his costs have increased considerably, because of all the things he's done for Scarlett. He is still operating at a profit, but his proportion of rewards to costs is getting slim at two to one. The relationship is now inequitable to Rhett's disadvantage and to Scarlett's considerable advantage. This inequity makes this a bad relationship, even though it is still profitable to both people.

After a few more days of fetching and carrying for Scarlett, Rhett recognizes the inequality that has resulted from all he's done for her. He resolves to restore balance to the relationship by getting more in return. After all, he figures she owes him.

The next day he asks Scarlett to help him work on the wording for his listing in the office's ad in the Sunday real estate supplement. He also asks her to talk to the office manager about getting his listings featured prominently in the ad. And, while she's talking to the office manager, would she also ask to have his desk moved so that he isn't stuck next to the coffee and rest rooms.

If Scarlett complies with all these requests, she can restore equity to the relationship. These behaviors would be costly to Scarlett, and would be of great reward value to Rhett. The two could return to an equitable four to one ratio.

Scarlett, however, is a busy woman. She's doesn't have time to waste writing ads, and she isn't going to spend her political capital with the office manager to get Rhett a new desk location. Feigning something urgent, which requires her immediate presence, she dashes from the office, while promising to get back in time to help Rhett. As she leaves, she asks him to do the computer runs for the "comparables" on two of her potential new listings so that she can determine the fair market price for the properties. Again, she explains that she likes to help new people, and this will be a way for Rhett to learn another aspect of the business. With that, she's gone with the wind.

It takes Rhett most of an hour to complete the data runs of the sales prices of recently sold homes comparable to Scarlett's two properties and, as he is compiling all the information, he reevaluates his relationship with Scarlett. He has just incurred even more costs, and because Scarlett hasn't returned to the office, he hasn't received the help he requested. Although he already has the information on the comparables, he decides to take the printout home with him, rather than laying it on her desk for her to find when she returns that evening.

Driving home he realizes his costs now actually exceed his rewards. He is operating at a loss. With all the time he has spent doing Scarlett's dirty work, he figures his ratio has reversed, and his costs are now twice as great as his rewards. Scarlett on the other hand, is profiting even more because she is closing deals while Rhett is doing her legwork.

When one person is profiting at the expense of another person's loss, the relationship has moved from inequitable to exploitive. A relationship is bad when it is inequitable even if it is still profitable. Now it's ugly, because it is inequitable and unprofitable for one person. Ms. O'Hara is exploiting Mr. Butler.

IN SEARCH OF EQUITY

You can apply this analysis to your existing relationships to help clarify why one relationship is good and why another is bad. To practice, pick two or three of your work relationships that you think of as good and one that you think of as bad. Write down the rewards you give the other person, the costs you incur, the rewards the other person gives you, and the costs he incurs. You need only put approximate values on the behaviors that get exchanged, but you will quickly see which relationships are equitable and profitable and which are inequitable to your disadvantage.

This analysis can help you pinpoint the changes you need to make to transform a bad relationship into a good one. Seeing these inequities in black and white probably makes you upset and kindles your desire to make some changes. What do you want to change? Obviously, you want the relationship to be equitable instead of inequitable. How can you achieve that? The relationship will become equitable if the other person gives you more rewards, or if you decrease your costs.

If what you want are more rewards, what specific behaviors do you want? More cooperation? More respect? More responsibility? Don't be satisfied with these high-altitude descriptions. Keep questioning yourself until you get to ground-level descriptions of the specific behaviors and outcomes you desire. It is fine to start with high-altitude words such as trust, respect, cooperation, understanding, initiative, and productivity, but to be effective you must translate each one into concrete actions you could ask the other person to perform.

The other change you could make to restore equity in a relationship would be to reduce some of your costs. Are you operating in the Rhett model of providing endless favors and assistance to someone who isn't reciprocating? If so, you might consider cutting back on all this free service. Here too you want to be specific about the behaviors that you want to stop doing.

Your goal is to identify the specific behavioral changes you could ask someone to make, or that you could make yourself, to transform a bad relationship into one that is equitable and profitable to both parties. The same applies for a group of workers who may perceive their relationship with their employer as inequitable. Their morale is low, and they are unhappy, but their best approach to improving their situation is to address the specific behaviors that are producing the negative feelings.

This analysis doesn't deny that people have feelings, but it suggests that the feelings are a result of whether or not the underlying behavioral exchange is equitable. This is why telling people to be happy doesn't have a lasting effect on their mood. The feelings result from the exchange, and it is only when the exchange is brought to a state of equity that the person's feelings will become positive.

The approach also illuminates the hundreds of studies designed to find the factors that make good leaders. None of the studies to date has clearly identified particular personal leadership traits or management styles as universally effective. Instead, the research shows that what people look for in a leader is a person who produces for them. In other words, matters of personality and style are secondary in comparison to whether or not the person treats his followers in a way that is equitable and profitable.

Reactions to Being in a Bad Relationship

People do more than get unhappy when they are in an inequitable relationship, they do something about it. What they do follows a fairly predictable pattern, which can be illustrated with the earlier example of inequity.

Before things went from bad to worse, Rhett decided to make some changes. If you were caught in an inequitable relationship as Rhett was, which number in your ratio of rewards and costs would you want to change first? Rhett, like most of us, tried first to increase his rewards. He asked Scarlett to assist him with his ads and to use her persuasive charms on the office manager to get him even more rewards. If Scarlett had followed through on her promises and done as she said she would, equity would have been restored to the relationship.

But Scarlett didn't perform as promised and thereby blocked Rhett's first attempt to restore equity. Frustrated in his attempt to gain more rewards, Rhett moved on to a second strategy. He did fewer things for Scarlett. He didn't give her the information on the comparables. He didn't bother to telephone her at the spa when those two important phone calls came in. In other words, he did everything possible to decrease his own costs.

Rhett's response was typical. In an inequitable relationship, the people on the losing end often do as little as possible and don't put out quality work. While reducing their costs, they're simultaneously reducing the rewards to their co-workers and supervisors. They're not doing this because they are angry, burned out, or feel unappreciated. They're decreasing their output to send a message and produce a change. They are unhappy, and they want the other person to do something about it. They want more rewards.

Most of us read the nonverbal message of discontent and ask the former good performer what's wrong. At first, he may say that it is nothing, but it won't take long before he tells you exactly what is wrong. We've all heard it before: "What's the use of knocking yourself out for someone who doesn't appreciate you?"

By now we know that he wants more than appreciation. He wants that appreciation to take a particular form, and if you give him the opportunity, he'll tell you. "I'd feel appreciated if you did a few good turns for me for a change." As he starts reading his wish list, you realize he doesn't want just your feelings of concern. He wants you to take actions that are rewarding to him. That is the reason he lowered his production. He is trying to prod you into making the relationship more profitable and equitable for him.

If reducing his costs and simultaneously reducing your rewards isn't enough to restore equity to the relationship, there is a third option—inflict costs on you.

Rhett, on his way home Friday evening, could drive by and take the key out of the lock box. This would mean that all the realtors who bring prospects by on Saturday wouldn't be able to get in. They would be furious with Scarlett, and she could miss a selling opportunity. Maybe he will give her the printout of the comparables after all, but in his analysis he'll pick "comparables" that lead to pricing the house way over market, so that it won't sell for months. Or, he could drop innuendoes when her clients call on the phone, like "We never know where she is or what she's doing. I'm not even sure she does. I'll put your message in her box with all the others." Or, "Oh, you work with Scarlett. I admire your patience and faith. Good luck."

When these costly acts are directed at the company, they are called sabotage. French workers in the industrial age would take their wooden shoes (sabots) and throw them into the machinery. "Oops. I hope that didn't hurt anything." In the computer age, unhappy workers still damage equipment, but they have something even better than sabots. They can throw an electronic monkey wrench into the computer and really foul up the works.

Employees can also exact costs by not coming to work on a day when they are really needed. It's even more costly if they don't give you any prior notice. When you finally call Anita at 9:30 A.M. to ask where she is, she adopts a raspy voice and says, "Oh, I'm dying here, but at least my voice is finally starting to come back. I **feel** so bad that I can't be there today. I'll try to come in this afternoon." She "feels" and she'll "try," but you are not getting rewarding behavior from her. Instead, her pattern of absenteeism is getting very costly to you.

If all these strategies prove ineffective in getting you to provide him with more rewards, the person will then move to terminate the relationship. In the exit interview, he may say he is leaving because he is unhappy, and indeed he is. But, there is an underlying reason why he is unhappy and that is because he perceives the relationship as extremely inequitable. It is his inability to return the relationship to one that is equitable and profitable that makes him leave. He'll leave when he finds a job he "likes better"—one that is more equitable and profitable.

Who's Counting?

The behavior exchange approach implies that at some level, whether consciously or unconsciously, people are keeping score. Many people don't want to believe this is true. It's true.

This assertion that people keep score should be qualified, however. As long as the relationship is equitable and profitable, people only keep rough score. If the relationship becomes inequitable and stays unbalanced for very long—and how would they know this if they had not been keeping tabs—people seem to keep track of every little thing.

Not only do people keep an accounting of their relationship with you, they audit your relationships with other people as well. You can tell someone's been counting when he says, "Well, it's all a matter of politics around here." Or, "Everyone knows that Kevin is your fair-haired boy and can do no wrong." Or, "Why do I always get all the dirty jobs? Why doesn't Lauren ever have to do this stuff?" On his scorecard, Kevin is getting all the rewards, Lauren never incurs any costs, and the lone scorekeeper is being treated inequitably.

This scorekeeping goes unnoticed in the best relationships because truly equitable relationships are akin to complete chemical reactions. When two reactive chemicals are first thrown together, we can usually see the reaction by color, form, or temperature change.

When the reaction is "complete," the combined chemicals appear unchanging. This is called chemical equilibrium. While it looks like nothing more is happening in chemical equilibrium, the reality is that the two chemicals are now interchanging electrons so rapidly, and so evenly, that the exchange is virtually invisible.

People keep track of the costs and rewards going back and forth in even the most personal of relationships. When are you unhappy with your mate? You get downright angry when you're doing the shopping, cleaning, cooking, house maintenance, and working nine-to-five, while your partner contributes nothing but an appetite. If the inequity is bad enough and goes on long enough, your marriage may come unglued.

While even family members and lovers keep track of the exchanges in their relationships, there is one major difference between business and personal relationships—the time element. In a business relationship, it is expected that inequities will be quickly restored to balance. If, as a consumer, you buy a product (a reward to you), you are expected to pay for it (the store owner's rewards) more or less immediately.

By contrast, "unpaid accounts" are tolerated for much longer in personal relationships. We've all had a friend, or family member, who was in a tough spot. The person may have been demanding a lot from us at a time when he or she was giving very few rewards in return. We may put up with this inequity for weeks, months, or even years. There is, however, a limit even in the best of relationships, when the practical economics of the exchange take precedence over loyalty, love, or gratitude. Gross inequities can eventually lead to estrangement.

Why Will People Treat You Equitably?

Assuming that you are attracted to the idea of having relationships that are equitable, how can you make certain that people are nice to you, that they treat you equitably, or fairly, rather than inequitably?

Try this as a multiple choice question.

A. People will treat you fairly because they are **good** people.
B. People will treat you fairly if you treat them fairly.
C. People will be nice to you because they have a conscience and would feel bad if they took advantage of you.

Answer A assumes the world has two kinds of people—good people, who always treat people equitably, and mean people who don't. If you only get involved with nice people, you'll always be treated equitably. The drawback to this assumption is that life is not that simple. No one, being human, is nice all the time. Situations change, and when they do, the way people treat you also changes.

Answer B assumes that your own fairness will prompt reciprocal fairness from everyone you meet. Unfortunately, a lot of people are willing to accept your generosity and feel no compulsion to return it. The sad truth is that the hand doing the feeding gets bitten all too often.

Answer C assumes that the world is populated by people with strict consciences and that feelings of guilt are a powerful cause of behavior. If guilt can make people behave so properly, then why do people feel so much guilt?

There is another answer. Assuming consequences cause behavior, it will be consequences that make people treat you equitably. Put bluntly, people will treat you fairly if you make it rewarding for them to do so.

The underlying assumption here is that whether your relationships are equitable or inequitable is very much within your own control. Make it in people's self-interest to treat you equitably, and you'll have balanced, equitable relationships. Make it pay for them to treat you inequitably, however, and they'll just do that. If you carry on a relationship in which you give and give and give without ever asking for anything in return, it's hardly surprising that the other person takes and takes and takes and the relationship winds up unbalanced.

Yes, it would probably be a better world if people were just automatically fair. But this world isn't that bad, because whether or not people treat you fairly is something you can control. You can let people treat you unfairly and be unhappy, or you can make it pay for people to treat you fairly. When you do create relationships that are equitable and profitable for you and the other person, you will both be satisfied.

Dealing with Problems in Relationships.

Most of us use a variety of indirect methods to cope with problems in our relationships. We often try to ignore the problem, hoping it will just go away. We may begin to avoid being around the person so we don't have to face the problem. If we can't avoid the individual, we can at least quit talking to him.

Another oblique approach is to talk about the problem, but to talk to other people rather than the actual source of the conflict. We hope they'll solve our problem for us, but they seldom bother. Sometimes we'll make dramatic shows of emotion to communicate our desire for change. Angry outbursts and sulking are equally ineffective in getting to a constructive solution. Snide and sarcastic comments in the person's presence are another common indirect means of communication. All of these indirect approaches do more to promote problems than to solve them.

A better way to deal with problems is to talk with the other person about the specific actions you would like him to take. Do not condemn, or use global indictments; instead, discuss only the actions you want him to change. We are so accustomed to relying on emotional and nonverbal communication that talking about the specific problem behavior almost seems like a radical idea. This direct approach won't necessarily eliminate all problems, but given the ineffectiveness of the indirect methods, it is well worth a try. Watch how it can work in a common problem situation.

The boss makes an assignment and the employee reacts with a dramatic huff of displeasure. In response, the boss gets angry because he thinks his request is reasonable and that the employee is simply trying to cause trouble. The employee angrily walks away, thinking the boss is too demanding. The assignment probably won't be done quickly or expertly, and may not get done at all. Both parties get emotional, but the problem remains.

What if the boss calmly asked a question or two before getting upset. Say you ask Danny to give you a report on the auditor's progress. He snorts and shakes his head as he turns to leave your office. Politely calling him back, you admit you haven't been around an ongoing audit for quite a while "From your reaction, I

sense that you and I view this assignment differently,"
you might say. "You seem to think that it will involve
much more work than I thought it would. I'm not sure
I really know exactly what would be involved for you,
and I wonder if you would be willing to take a minute
or two to help me understand exactly what you think
would be involved?"

If you remain calm, some startling things will happen as Danny tells you what he thinks you are asking
him to do. First, as Danny goes into detail about the
number of hours and effort involved in compiling a
report at this stage of the audit, you may realize that
you had no idea just how big a demand you were
making. Once you realize how time-consuming and
costly the report will be, you'll no doubt decide to
modify your request, or offer to provide him with some
assistance.

Second, you may realize that Danny has overinter-
preted your request. You just wanted a global statement of progress, and a rough estimate of the completion date, but he thinks you want a detailed account of
each phase of the audit, which would take him hours.
You'll quickly understand that Danny got upset because he misunderstood what you wanted him to do.
Once you understand his perceived costs, it is easy to
let Danny know that your request was actually much
more limited.

By talking down at ground level, in unemotional
terms, it is usually possible to resolve differences in the
values people place on behavior and thereby solve most
problems. When someone is good enough to explain
exactly how they interpret a request, be sure to thank
them for their willingness to communicate in this direct and constructive manner.

QUID PRO QUO

This "give and take" exchange is an ongoing part of all our work relationships. A job itself, for instance, is essentially an agreement in which the employee trades his work for salary and other benefits. In personal relationships, the exchange is often implicit, whereas in business relationships it usually involves candid discussion of what will be traded. In either case, you use the process of trading to produce change. You want other people to take actions that will produce rewards for you, and they want you to do things that will result in rewards for them. So you trade what you have for the actions you want from others. Quid pro quo is Latin for "something for something." In everyday parlance it means "I'll do this for you, if you will do that for me."

This notion of making trades should not be misinterpreted as meaning that you never do anything for someone unless you get something tangible back immediately. There are many small favors and requests for assistance we grant without condition. If someone asks to borrow your pen, you don't ask for a paper clip in return. If, however, the request is for a much more costly favor, then you can use the opportunity to make a trade for something of comparable value in return.

If you want to give things away to other people for free, that is entirely your prerogative. You should, however, refrain from later complaining about the person's ingratitude in not returning the favor. Keep in mind that you influence the trades in your relationships, so if you make it pay for people to treat you inequitably, you have no one to blame but yourself.

You may be wondering why you have to offer a trade, when you are only asking the person to do the job for which you are paying him. As much as you may resent the idea of the trading process, consider your alternatives. You have already talked to the person several times without success, and repeated attempts at guidance, counseling, or persuasion are unlikely to produce results. What more can you do? Threaten him? Dismiss him? Give up? Threats will only aggravate the situation, giving up gets you nowhere, and dismissal, while tempting, isn't always a realistic possibility. The person is often too valuable to fire, and it would be expensive and time-consuming to find a comparable replacement.

When the normal techniques haven't worked, and you must produce change, try the exchange approach. Many of the rewards you will now be offering to trade are things that you have probably been giving away free, so it isn't actually going to cost you that much. And it's a technique that produces measurable results.

The Ethics of Trading

For some people, the idea of making trades to get other people to do what they want seems overly controlling and somehow wrong. The ethics of this approach deserve to be addressed, because what may appear suspect is actually very ethical.

When someone asks you for a sizable favor, they are essentially asking you to incur a large cost and to give them a reward. Assuming the relationship was equitable up to this point, their request will have the effect of making the relationship inequitable, and specifically to your disadvantage. When you then propose a trade in return, you are merely restoring the relationship to its prior equitable status.

The strategies for making trades, and the specific

techniques to be described later in this book, can be
viewed as tools for shaping relationships. When viewed
in this way, these techniques can be judged along the
same lines as any tool or device. How do we assess the
goodness or badness of an automobile or a computer?
When an automobile carries someone to lifesaving
health care, we judge it to be good. But when we think
of the thousands and thousands of people who die in
auto accidents each year, we consider whether we
might be better off without cars. In the same way, the
computer is good when it saves us hours of tedious
work, and it is terrible when a malfunction requires us
to do hours of tedious work to correct the problem.

From this perspective, ethical goodness, or badness, is not intrinsic to the tool, but is determined by
the quality of the outcomes that result from its use.
Both cars and computers have the potential to create
positive and negative consequences. The same is true
of the tools we use in interpersonal relationships. They
can produce positive results—equitable and profitable
relationships; or they can produce very negative results—inequitable and exploitive relationships.

Getting Started

If you haven't systematically been making trades, you
may be in for some interesting surprises once you start.
People's initial reaction may be astonishment and
shock, and some may even say unflattering things
about you. The first time you propose a quid pro quo
trade rather than a free lunch, you may hear remarks
like, "What do you mean? Are you saying you won't
help me unless I do something for you? That's not very
nice." Or, "What's happened to you? You used to be

so easygoing. Now everything is a trade." Or, "I used to think that you were different, but now I see that you're just like all the other self-centered types around here. Everything is a matter of what's in it for me. I liked the old you a lot better than this version."

Don't worry now about how to respond to this resistance. Subsequent chapters will describe simple sentences you can use to deflect these remarks. Think instead about why people are reacting so negatively. They liked you the old way because you used to give your resources away for free. Even though you privately hoped for reciprocation, you seldom asked for it. The old you created relationships which were inequitable to other people's advantage. Now they want you to return to that old way—the way that served their self-interest. Their negative reactions are little warnings that, if you keep proposing trades, then they will inflict a cost on you, which will be their disdain and dislike. They are also implicitly promising that if you return to your give-away program, they will restore the reward of their acceptance and expressions of liking.

If you stick to your guns and keep suggesting trades, you have wonderful surprises ahead. The people accustomed to your free lunch will be disarmed initially, and they may even resist your requests two or even three times. But about the fourth time, you are going to hear something very startling. The accountant who always tries to sneak out at 4 o'clock on Friday might say, "I'd like to leave work an hour early tomorrow, and I know what you are going to say. You're going to ask for something in return, so here's what I propose. If you'll let me leave early, I'll teach the new trainee how to process the delinquent accounts on my own time."

That's right. They'll propose the trade. Once people get used to your new style, and once they learn they can't frighten you back to the old way, they will come in the door and offer you an exchange. You can just sit back and decide whether or not you like their proposal. Often they'll suggest doing things for you that you never would have had the courage to ask for. Try it and let it work for you.

Many managers hesitate to start making trades because they fear that people won't like them. These managers don't pause to ask whether the people who like them so much also respect them. Generally, managers who don't make trades aren't well-respected by their subordinates or their peers. They are viewed as weak—nice but more than a little naive.

Consider, too, the impression you are making on your superiors. If you let others walk all over you, the big guys will see you as incapable of managing people. If they were to give you more responsibility, it would just mean that more people would be getting away with murder. Your failure to systematically make these trades may win you the temporary adoration of those who benefit from your largess, but it may also block your chances for promotion and advancement.

The exchange process is designed to help you create equitable and profitable relationships and defend against exploitation. Using it, you can quickly and constructively make changes that benefit everyone involved—and that is the secret of the trade.

C H A P T E R   F O U R

The World's Most Persuasive Communication

With most employees, you can spontaneously make a reasonable request, and they will go along with it. But, when your previous three or four requests to one individual in particular have been met with repeated resistance, your frustration may lead you to wish you could fire the resistor. Despite its emotional appeal, termination usually ends up being very costly. Before you resort to such an extreme approach, talk to him once more, but this time plan your change strategy more deliberately. This planning doesn't have to be very complicated. It's all a matter of fitting your request into a simple but powerful communication format and then selecting the best time.

TWO LITTLE WORDS

Every successfully persuasive communication depends on two key words. Whether they're used in a slick magazine to get you to buy a new sports car, by a politician stumping for votes, or by a salesperson touting mutual funds, the message remains the same: "If you will take this action, then you'll get this reward." The two crucial words are IF and THEN.

This is a contingency. The "IF" half of this sentence states the actions that must be taken and the "THEN" half describes the consequences of that action. The contingency is the world's most persuasive communication, and it is used time and time again to induce change. Every effective persuasive message you've ever encountered is a restatement of an "if . . . , then . . ." proposition.

Look at the classic magazine ad for a Corvette sports car. What color is the car? Red. Is it a hard top or convertible? Convertible. Who is sitting in the passenger seat? A beautiful woman. What is the message? IF you perform the desired behavior and buy the car, THEN you will get this reward—the attention of a beautiful person.

Advertisers use this contingency all the time. If you buy my detergent, then your laundry will be the envy of the neighborhood. If you buy this cereal, then you'll enjoy eternally youthful good health. If you watch this news program, then you'll be the most informed person in the car-pool.

The use of the contingency for change isn't just restricted to selling goods. The politician addressing the gathered supporters talks to them about the flag, mom, apple pie, and the bright new future ahead. Inside the hyperbole, what's the message? "IF you take this action and vote for me, THEN you will get better services and lower taxes."

You can use the two-word format of the contingency, too. It will be the most powerful tool you can use for persuading people to change their behavior. The more closely your change request is modeled after the if-then format, the more likely you are to get people to do what you want.

Knowing What You Want

In preparing to make a change request you should first determine exactly what behavior you want from the other person. This requires nothing more than describing the changes you want in ground-level language.

If you say to Harry, "I wish you weren't so negative at those department meetings," how is Harry likely to react? He might give you a look that clearly indicates that he questions your sanity, he might roll his eyes in disgust and walk away, or he might treat you to a full-blown explanation of why he isn't more positive, but he's unlikely to change.

If, on the other hand, you are very specific and say to Harry, "I want you to smile and say one positive thing about the production department at the beginning of the weekly planning meeting," you've dramatically increased the likelihood that he will do what you want. Harry now clearly knows the basic behavior you are seeking. Make your request for change in precise ground-level language to maximize your effectiveness.

Maybe you want Harry not only to smile and make positive remarks, but to use the meetings as a time to share his insights into the company's future production and to learn from the salespeople what new products and services the customers want. You'd also like him to encourage more frequent communication between his design group and that sales group. And, while you're at it, you figure it wouldn't kill him to leave his office door open once in a while so that people feel free to approach him with questions.

That's a long list of changes you want. Nothing of lasting value was ever created in a hurry and, outside of fairy tales, no frog has turned into a prince overnight. You can transform behavior, but you have to concentrate on changing one thing at a time. When you are preparing to ask for change, choose one behavioral change to ask for at a time.

If you try to change too many things at once, you'll increase the chances of getting resistance, and decrease your chances of producing any change. This week, ask Harry to attend the luncheon meeting and make one positive statement. Next week, ask him to tell the group about his current project. The following week, get him to talk to the salespeople and identify three new things that the customers are requesting.

When you are working with a person from whom you want a number of behavioral changes, keep the first two or three changes small. Get them accustomed to your new approach and let them understand that you are serious about it. Once that is established, you can start asking for bigger changes. Very often, after the first few small changes, you'll get a dramatic transformation. After they learn that you've changed, and that you're going to enforce your contingencies, they'll switch to your new method, and begin readily making changes to get what they want.

The key to achieving this kind of transformation is sticking to your contingency. People use resistance to get you to withdraw your request. The purpose of the resistance is to undermine your contingency, and later chapters will show you how to easily circumvent this resistance. If you consistently stick to the terms of your contingency, people will soon learn that they will have to make the changes you want to get the rewards they want.

Knowing What They Want

Once you've specified what one behavioral change you're going to ask for, the next step is to scan your resources for something you can offer in exchange. A resource can be anything you have that someone else wants. Semantically, the name changes from a resource to a reward when it's offered to another person as part of the change contingency.

The more specific you are about the benefits the other person will receive, the more likely you are to get the behavior change. If you say to Harry, "If you'll smile and say one positive thing at the beginning of the meeting, it'll make my day," Harry might do it. Then again, what exactly does making your day do for Harry?

If, on the other hand, you use ground-level language for both parts of your contingency, Harry will most likely perform the desired behavior. "Harry, if you'll smile and say one positive thing about the production department at the beginning of the meeting, then I'll be happy to talk to the group about increasing their recycling efforts for five minutes at the end of the meeting so you won't have to do it."

Now Harry has a concrete incentive to make the change you are requesting. He's been griping about his fellow managers' slack approach to recycling, and he's asked you to do something about it. To get the change you want in the meeting, you're offering to do something that you know is a direct reward for him.

This appeal is critical. When you are identifying a resource to offer as a reward, make certain it's something that has specific reward value to the person whose behavior you want to change.

The next chapter will help you identify the many resources you have at your disposal. Many people think they don't have any resources, or at least none of a sufficient weight to prompt anyone to change. You'll discover you've been overlooking a wealth of potential resources that can be offered as rewards for change.

Now that your contingency for change is carefully prepared, you have to decide when to use it. As in comedy and so much of life, timing is everything.

When to Make Requests

If you stop and think about it, it's really no wonder that so many of our requests are ignored. Our timing is atrocious. Most of us pick the worst possible moment to ask for things, the one moment when we are least likely to get them. Watch what we do.

"Amy, could you do me a favor?"

"Gee, Joe, I really need your help right now."

"Look, Lucinda, I'm desperate. Could you help me out?"

We almost always make our requests when we need something. That is the worst possible time. If you make a request when you are in need, you are in a low power position. The other person has a resource you want, so that other person has the power. You are dependent on him. He can decide just how much you'll have to pay to get what he has. And the more you want it, the more you'll have to pay to get it.

If the worst possible time to ask for something is when the other person has something you want, when is the best possible time to ask? The best possible time to ask is when the other person needs something from you.

You are in the high power position when you have what other people want. You have the resource the persistent resistor needs, and that resource is going to become the reward in the "then" part of your contingency.

It's easy to know when people need something from you. They'll ask for it.

"Will you do me a favor?"

"Do you mind if I leave a little early Friday?"

"Could you hold off on that?"

"Do we have to do all of these reports?"

We usually greet such requests for favors with caution. We're used to viewing these requests as demands that are going to cost us time and money. Perhaps you should rethink your approach and begin to use these requests as golden opportunities to get the changes you want.

Other people's requests are signals telling you that you're in the high power position. Greet them with a smile. The person asking you for a favor has just handed you the chance you've been waiting for, the perfect time to make your request for change.

As soon as you hear a request, acknowledge it, and immediately ask for something in return.

"Bill, I'd be happy to do that. And you know, there's something you could for me as well. If you'll push out the Simpson's order by noon, I'll be happy to give you an extra three days to file this report."

"Sure, Robin, I'm confident we can work out a way for you to leave early Friday. How about this? If you'll see that those expense vouchers are processed by five today, I'll be happy to let you out of here at 4 on Friday."

Once said, be quiet! Saying and doing nothing after you propose a trade is crucial when dealing with a persistent resistor. Avoid explaining why you want to make a trade, why the trade is fair, or why the other person should accept the trade.

Just state the trade, smile, and wait for their agreement. At the most, add "All right?" or "Okay?" When they say yes, you've got the fair deal you wanted.

Is It Okay to Propose a Trade?

Responding to requests by immediately asking for a trade may, at first, seem too overtly manipulative, but look at the transaction in terms of the exchange analysis. When someone asks you to do something for them, they are asking you to incur a cost and to give them a reward. Their request therefore creates an inequity in what was an equitable relationship.

If you agree to incur the cost and pay out the reward without asking for something in return, you're simply being a party to fostering an inequity in the relationship. An inequity that is to your disadvantage. If, on the other hand, you immediately ask for something of comparable value in return, you are restoring the equity in the relationship.

Remember the earlier discussion of why people will treat you fairly. People treat each other equitably because it is in their own best interest to do so. That is just what you are doing when you take the initiative and propose fair trades that restore equity to your relationships.

How Big a Favor?

The magnitude of the favor you request should be proportional to the other's request. If someone asks for something small, the behavior change you ask for in return will be small. When Sissy, the receptionist, asks to extend her lunch break by five minutes, you can ask her to thoroughly clean the glass surface on the office copying machine. When someone makes a larger, more costly request, then make what you ask for in return comparably larger. If Sissy wants to leave an hour early every Thursday for the next twelve weeks to get to a night class on time, you could reasonably ask her to come in one Saturday morning a month for each of the next three months.

Once you begin to use the principle of equity in proposing trades, you'll find you want people to ask you for big favors. The bigger, the better, because the more they ask of you, the more you ask for and expect to get in return.

What If They Say No?

People won't always agree to your proposed trade, especially at first. They're used to getting something for nothing so they may express surprise, shock, perhaps even a trace of disgust as they reject your offer. Don't take this no as final. In fact, you might act as though you didn't even hear it and simply restate the trade: "Here's what I'm proposing, Robin. If you get the expense vouchers processed by five tomorrow, then you can leave work an hour early on Friday. Okay?"

If they say no again, describe the full situation for them once more: "You've asked me to help you, and I'm asking for something in return. That's only fair. What do you say? Can we cooperate on this?"

If they still say no, then you're going to have to say no to their request. Do it politely. You might even express regret that you weren't able to work out an agreement. Some people keep saying no to get you to give in to their request without having to give you anything in return. After testing you, discovering that the rules of the game have changed, and learning that the free lunch is no longer available, they'll start coming around.

What If They Say It's Not Fair?

If the person tells you that the offered trade isn't fair, use specification to get to terms to which both of you can agree. Politely ask him to describe specifically the costs associated with the actions you're requesting. You can do this by saying, "Well, I want this to be fair. Maybe I've misjudged things. Would you mind describing what would be involved for you?"

You may very likely find that the other person thinks you are asking them to do a whole lot more than you actually want them to do. Unless you've been very specific about what you want them to do, the other person may be making some false assumptions.

Your colleague John comes to your office with a smile and asks if he can borrow one of your staffers for an hour to provide some clerical help with an important rush project. "Sure, John," you say. "I'd be happy to give you the clerical help you need. But do you think you could help me with something? Could you give the Thursday planning group a recap of the training session we attended last week?"

John cries no-fair and you ask why.

"All I'm asking for is an hour's worth of extra clerical help," he laments. "You're asking me to undertake three extra hours of work. Do you have any idea how long it's going to take me to recreate the charts they used, get copies of the manual, and organize the whole thing?"

Obviously, you haven't been specific enough. All you really want is a brief oral overview of the class. Once you specify that, the two of you should be able to quickly reach an agreement.

If you have asked for too much, asking the other person to spell out exactly what will be involved for him enables you to readjust your request so that it is fair. But, be careful that resistors don't use this discussion of the fairness of the trade to avoid changing. Just as Sancho Panza could never find the right tree to be hanged from, resistors are never quite satisfied with the proposed trade. Panza avoided hanging; they avoid changing.

What If You're Not Ready?

Once in a while, someone is going to ask you for something and he or she will catch you unprepared. If someone's just hit the ball to your side of the net, you have two options that will still allow you to make the change you want.

First, you can give a tentative agreement and ask

for time to consider their request. This will give you the chance to think of just what changes you'd like from this person.

"I think I can go along with that, Laura. I just need some time to trace out the implications of doing it. Can I get back to you at three this afternoon?"

You've tentatively agreed to meet their request and promised a firm answer in a short time. Anticipating that they'll get what they want, people will give you time to think. You can use that time to determine what would make an equitable trade. When you have figured out what would be fair, then go to the person and propose the exchange.

Your second choice is to get an IOU. You can agree to give the other person what they've asked for, if the person will promise to do something for you in the future. Almost everyone will agree to this kind of an exchange because all they are giving away are good intentions, not costly behaviors.

If you accept an IOU, trade it in quickly. IOU's tend to depreciate very rapidly. If you let more than a day or two pass between the time someone gives you an IOU and the time you call it in, you're likely to get nothing but regret and more promises.

"Wow, Fred, I'm so sorry I can't help you out with that right now. If only you'd asked me yesterday, I would have been happy to do that. My situation should improve by the end of the month. Check with me then."

It's best not to be caught flatfooted. You'll be able to use people's requests for favors to greater advantage if you've planned in advance exactly what behavior changes you want from other people.

People will come to you with their requests at unexpected times, so it's critical to be prepared. Look at the important people around you. Draw up a wish list of all the specific actions you'd like from them. Wait until they come to you with their requests. Then, you'll be ready to trade for the changes you want.

Chances are, you won't have to wait very long. Subordinates always want things from you. They have long lists of things you have that they want. No waiting here. Peers want things from you on a fairly regular basis, so the waiting time will be relatively short. Superiors may come asking for *special* favors infrequently. As every manager, supervisor, crew chief, or boss of any stripe knows, however, there are times when they can't survive without some extra effort from their subordinates.

The really smart subordinates—and you may have some and you can learn to be one—know exactly what a crisis in the workplace is. A crisis is when the boss really, really needs them. A crisis is when a person who is usually in a low power position is suddenly in a high power position.

Crisis or not, you have to fulfill your usual job requirements without trying to use performance of them as a bargaining chip, so if your superior is simply asking you to do the job you were hired to do, you've got nothing to trade. However, if you watch, crises small and large will come. Maybe your superior wants work done much quicker than usual, maybe he wants extra work done, maybe he needs something done in a special way. These are the times when you can ask for the things you want, but always make your request of comparable value to what is being asked of you.

Be prepared. Know what you want from your superiors so that when these occasions arise, you can take the opportunity to get the specific changes you desire.

When you are making an exchange with a superior, your manner and tone should be deferential. When you are trading with a superior, you must indicate that you recognize the superior's position. You can do this both explicitly and implicitly.

Explicitly, you acknowledge their higher position and quickly agree with their request.

"Sure boss, I'd be happy to help you."

Or, "Anything you say. I'd be glad to do it."

Implicitly, you communicate the recognition of the chief's superior position by using qualifying phrases and proposing your requests as questions.

"Would you be willing to . . . ?"

"I was wondering if . . . ?"

"What would you think of . . . ?"

"Would it be all right if . . . ?"

The full statement in an actual situation might be: "Sure chief, I'll be glad to come in this weekend and work on it. Say, I was wondering if you would be willing to consider an idea of mine. Could I possibly use a couple of days next week and work exclusively on developing that reorganization plan I proposed?"

Such deference and qualification is not as necessary when exchanging with subordinates and peers. In these cases your request is a simple declarative sentence, but with a superior it's more tentatively stated as a question.

With superiors, your initial request might just hint at a link between what they are asking for and what you are asking for. Your deferential manner suggests that accepting this linkage is entirely up to the boss.

If you're in a stronger position, you don't have to be as tentative. Try to state your request without qualifiers. If you sense irritation when you do this, then back off a bit, and restate your request with the qualifiers, "Could you possibly?" "Is there a chance?" "I was wondering if you might?"

You can gradually increase the forcefulness of your proposal to your superior. If you don't get what you want the first time around, you can make the link stronger the second time around.

"Sure, Gene, I'll get those numbers run for you before the auditors arrive, and could I take two days next week to flesh out that reorganization idea I proposed?"

The language here is a little less submissive and the link between his request for numbers and yours for time to work on your proposal is more direct.

The third time around you may have to be pretty direct. You can emphasize the cost he is asking you to incur and the value of what he wants, and can remind him of your prior requests that have gone unheeded.

"You want me to run these numbers by tomorrow? Boy, I'm really going to have to push to get them done by then. I can see how important it could be to have those summary figures at your fingertips for the executive committee meeting in the morning. Clearly, it could be embarrassing if the people in finance started asking questions. Sure, I'll gladly stay late tonight and do it for you. Could you return the favor by letting me use next Wednesday and Thursday to work exclusively on my reorganization plan?"

This direct link should get the change you desire.

Another Bad Time to Ask

Trying to make an exchange when you're in need and consequently in a low power position is the very worst time to ask for something. There is another bad time to watch out for—right after you have given away your resources.

"Oh, nice suit, Larry. Your wife buy that for you? You know, she has the most marvelous taste. Here, let me get that for you. By the way, I typed and made copies of your reports. I know you didn't ask, but I thought that might make things easier for you. Say, do you mind if I borrow the company car during lunch to run a couple of errands?"

This is the classic low power strategy. The logic is that if you can put Larry in a good mood by doing little things for him, then he'll feel grateful and will cheerfully grant your request.

This is usually a mistake. First of all, you've given away a number of things you could have exchanged with Larry. He no longer needs to ask you to type and copy the reports because you've already done it. You gave him your resource, and you haven't yet gotten anything in return. If he turns down your request to borrow the company car, where does that leave you? By giving away your assistance and your extra work, without getting something in return, you've created an inequity, and it is working to your disadvantage.

You've also made the mistake of counting on Larry's presumed feelings of gratitude. You've based it on the hope that his feelings will cause him to do what you think is right.

If Larry is in a strong position, he may feel grateful but that won't be enough to get him to go along with your request. He may even say that he feels guilty that he can't help you out. His feelings don't do you any good. You want action.

To keep your relationship with Larry equitable and profitable, keep your requests straightforward. Be patient, wait until Harry wants something from you, and make a fair trade with him to get what you want.

If and Only If

When using a contingency to change the behavior of a resistor, it's critical that the IF-THEN order be maintained. The person has to perform the action described in the "if" half before receiving the reward described in the "then" half. If this sequence isn't followed, the contingency loses all of its power.

Many people, particularly those attracted by the reward you're offering, will try to talk you into giving them the reward before they take the action you want. These resistors act like a smart horse who has some carrots dangling in front of his nose.

You are saying to the horse, "If you'll give me a lift to the next ranch, I'll give you these carrots."

The horse says, "I'm awfully tired, so I'll tell you what. Give me the carrots now, and then I'll have the energy to take you there."

Don't fall for this. The reward should be given only after the desired behavior is performed. Keep those carrots until the end of the ride. Resistors will often test you to see if they can get your resources for free. It may take a couple of encounters before they understand that the only way to get the reward you're offering is to give you something in return. Once they do, they'll go right along with the equitable trades you propose.

By knowing in advance exactly what behaviors you want, when to ask for them, and what to offer in return, you'll be prepared to make the changes you want. By the same token, asking for these changes as part of an exchange where you give something in return for everything you get, you'll be creating relationships that are equitable and trades that are profitable for both parties.

CHAPTER FIVE

Your Hidden Motivational Resources

You're all set to start trading for the specific changes you want. You know that the time to ask is when you've got something other people want. And there, you think, is the rub.

You haven't got anything your co-workers want. You're high enough up the ladder to be shouldering responsibility, but too low on it to have any authority. You don't set wages. You can't offer promotions. And, you can't fire anybody.

You think you're bankrupt, penniless, broke right down to the seams of your empty pockets. Hidden from your view, however, are hundreds of motivational resources your co-workers want. What's more, they're telling you what those assets are every single day.

Every time someone comes to you for a favor, they

are alerting you to one of your hidden motivational resources. By simply paying attention to what people request, you can begin to compile a list of the assets you possess. Knowing what you have in your inventory will make trading much easier. Here are some of the types of resources over which you may have decision-making discretion.

Bending the Rules

You haven't even finished unpacking your briefcase Monday morning when Michael, one of your employees, pokes his nose into your office.

"Gee, Lou," Michael says, "I got tied up Friday afternoon and forgot we had a meeting this morning, so I still haven't gotten last week's tally finished. I know I'm supposed to have that by noon, but would it be okay if I got it in tomorrow instead?"

A few minutes later as you walk down the hall for a cup of coffee, Greta, a colleague from another department stops you. "Look, I know the pool cars are supposed to be reserved for sales only, but my car is in the shop, and I've got to pick my mother-in-law up at the airport tonight. Would it be okay if I took a car home overnight?"

It's not even 9 o'clock Monday morning and your co-workers have already identified a cluster of resources you possess. You have the power to bend certain rules. Some rules can't be broken, of course, because even bending them could endanger people's safety or interfere with larger corporate goals. There are others, however, that are flexible.

You may be able to let Michael off the hook on the twelve o'clock deadline if he agrees to call the legal department to see what is holding up their opinion on the new contract forms. You may be able to trade Greta the use of a pool car tonight in exchange for her strong public support of your flex-time proposal at the next department head's meeting. You may be able to overlook minor violations, warn someone instead of writing them up, skip enforcement on occasion, or interpret the rules in the employee's favor. When co-workers come to you asking for these favors, your ability to accommodate them is a resource you can exchange for behavioral changes you want.

Scheduling

The night-shift supervisor is standing at your desk, asking once again for the next opening on the day shift. You have Joan's written request to schedule her vacation time during the last two weeks of June laying in front of you. The front desk clerk wants to know if she can take extended lunch breaks for the next three Tuesdays so she can attend a lecture series.

Your ability to make adjustments in work shifts, to negotiate flexibility in schedules, to give vacation days at peak request times is a huge resource. Having time to pursue other activities, or the flexibility to rearrange work schedules is a very valuable reward to many people. Don't underestimate its value if you can make decisions about people's schedules.

You may be able to honor Joan's request for two weeks off, just as the fiscal year is closing, in exchange for an early deadline on a public relations campaign she's been procrastinating about. You may be able to exchange longer lunch breaks for the job description and procedures' manual you have been requesting of the front desk clerk. The night supervisor's petition requires greater consideration.

If someone asks to change shifts, consider whether the request is for a temporary, or permanent change. If the night-shift supervisor wants to shift to days just for the week he has houseguests coming, that's a minor request and can be exchanged for a minor change. Make it clear during the discussion, however, that the switch in shifts is strictly temporary.

A permanent schedule change is a much more valuable resource than a temporary one. If you're going to make the change permanent, make certain you'll be getting something in return that is equal in significance. Once something is traded permanently, it's difficult to call it back, or reclaim it.

Assistance

Even if you're fairly low on the corporate totem pole, you're undoubtedly still asked for little favors all day long. Being the office manager isn't drawing you an impressive salary or world renown, but it is still giving you control over a number of resources other people want.

"Lou, can I borrow two of the clerical employees Friday morning so my group can get its presentation finished?"

"Lou, can you ask one of the secretaries to make my reservations when she makes yours? I hate holding for the airlines."

"Have you gotten any hints about how to make this report more palatable to accounting?"

"Do you mind if I commandeer the conference room this afternoon? I've got so many transparencies to review that they're overflowing my work station."

"Will you proofread this for me?"

These requests all seem minor, and denying any of them might make you feel like the grinch. But you don't have to. Many of the changes you want are also minor. Simply trade a small favor for a small change. When Debbie wants you to send a fax for her, you might ask her to double-check an invoice for you. If Jeff asks you to bring him a sandwich back from the cafeteria, you might ask him to call the purchasing department and check the status of your purchase order for a computer monitor.

Work Assignments

Another lode of resources can be discovered by listening to the wishful thinking subordinates express. Next time you walk to a meeting or share lunch with your employees, pay attention to their not-so-idle conversation.

"It would be so much fun if just once Paul and I were assigned to the same project again. We haven't worked together since we were both new employees."

"This stuff is so boring. I'd give my eye-teeth for an assignment with a little variety to it."

"I wish I were in Julie's group. Working on hotel decor is sure a lot more fun than color-coordinating another office complex."

"I know I could do that job if somebody would just give me the chance."

These wishful, and sometimes slightly envious comments, reveal a category of resources intrinsic to almost any management position. You have the power to assign your staff members to jobs with some novelty attached, or to projects with other benefits. You can team people up with their friends. You can give someone a job experience that makes them more promotable. Even an assignment to a tough position can be an asset to an employee who wants to prove herself.

An organization's seniority policies, or labor contract, may reduce a manager's resources. If employees get certain benefits simply by putting in their time, those benefits lose much of their value as motivational resources. It is only those resources over which you have discretion that can legitimately be made contingent upon performance.

Independence

If you control the degree of independence with which your subordinates pursue their work, then you have another set of resources. Many employees will gladly alter certain aspects of their current performance in exchange for greater independence.

If Dirk, usually a good-natured and flexible employee who is performing well in his assigned duties, keeps grousing about the standard deadlines for work performance, maybe you can let him set his own timetables in exchange for incorporating an extra reporting function into his current responsibilities. Can you offer increased decision-making opportunities? The leadership position on a group project? The go-ahead to pursue a pet project? Both you and your company benefit when you let an employee put his or her own idea to work.

When Mary comes to you with an idea for improvement that she'd like to pursue, hear her out. If you think her idea may have merit, give her a chance to develop it, but make the opportunity part of a contingency for change.

"Mary, that's an interesting concept, but I'll need to see a lot more detail, and even then I'm not certain I'd agree to it. To seriously consider it, I'd need a complete report that includes cost and time projections, savings expectations, and a work-flow plan. How about this? If you can complete each week's assignments by Thursday, then you can use the next four Fridays to work on your idea. When it's complete you can bring it to me for my reconsideration."

Who benefits here? Your company does; it gets the benefit of this employee's independent enterprise. You do; you get the benefit of work completed ahead of schedule and potentially a new cost-saving idea. The employee does; she gets the opportunity to make a contribution that could well affect her advancement and make her own job more satisfying. All in all, you're giving away very little and getting a great deal in return.

Formal Activities

As you peruse your calendar for a mutually convenient time for you and Arnold, your project architect, to review an ongoing project, you find that the days you had hoped to spend at the project site are taken for a convention in Atlanta.

"You going to the NDA convention? Is the OMNI team going to be there? I'd love to meet those people in person," says Arnold.

While you may view yet another out-of-town meeting as an irritation, a number of activities that are carried on in the name of business outside of the usual office, or industrial setting, carry a great deal of appeal for co-workers who don't routinely travel for business.

Employees may see it as a chance to travel, meet others in their industry, make new connections, and enjoy socializing. Listen to those comments, and recognize that they are telling you about more of your resources.

Remember, timing the use of a resource can be as important as matching the right resource to the right person. While attending the annual convention might have appealed to Mary last year, it may be a burden three months after she's had a new baby. Harrison who usually avoids traveling assiduously might gladly go to the convention in Orlando because he could conveniently spend the weekend with his retired parents in St. Petersburg. Or, he might be trying to accumulate some frequent flier miles right now. Keep up to date with people's changing needs. Matching your resources to people's needs is simply smart marketing.

Education

Louise, your marketing director, has been dodging your request for an expanded "existing-customer" program for weeks. You'd like to try a trade with her, but you can't think of a single thing you've got that she'd want. Then one day, the mail brings an answer.

Louise comes prancing into your office with a glossy brochure in her hand. "Hey, the AMA is offering a six-week course here in town for appraiser's certification," she announces. "They usually only offer this in Boston. This would be an easy way for me to get that certification."

Louise has given you a clue to another resource you can offer in exchange for behavior. Your willingness to fund job-related education for employees can be a great incentive for change. You may be able to authorize tuition assistance, okay time off to pursue courses, provide access to company-sponsored training programs, cross-training, informal coaching sessions, or monitoring. The employee will benefit from becoming more promotable, and you will benefit from their additional skills.

Perks

When you selected Gary for the new sales management position, did he want to talk about his expanded responsibilities? Absolutely not. He was more concerned with making certain that all the requisite perks came attached to the new position.

"I imagine we'll project a better company image to our clients if I show up in a respectable-looking car, don't you think?" he hinted not-so-subtly. "Except for the West-Coast customers, of course. I'll have to fly out there for those calls. I'll get to fly business-class instead of coach now, right?"

Travel opportunities, membership dues, company cars, expense accounts are all examples of perks that many people think simply come with certain job positions. These perks can be turned into motivational resources if you reserve them as rewards for change. Don't make that company car an automatic part of landing the regional sale's job.

To Gary's innuendo you might respond, "Oh, I agree. A nice car can contribute to creating a high profile. If you can increase sales by 15 percent in the next six months, I'll see that you get one for the next year."

Second, don't make the perks permanent. Notice that you're only offering the car to Gary for one year.

Similarly, you can make business-class air travel contingent upon certain behaviors. Tell Gary that if he brings the midwestern district's sales in line with your projections, you'll see that he flies business-class for the rest of the quarter.

You can also use these kinds of resources to achieve long-term goals. If Tom comes and says wistfully that he'd love to have a company car like Gary, that's the time to sit him down and find out what he is willing to do to get a company car. Help him work out a long-term action plan, so that by achieving each successive goal he can obtain the larger goal he wants. Remember that big rewards have big price tags and often take a long time to earn. If the prize is valuable enough, people will happily pay a big price to get it.

Coalitions

Three days before your company's executive committee meets to consider the new benefits package, your colleagues begin dropping by your office with increasing frequency.

"You know, Norm, your support of the new health care proposal could be crucial. Have you thought about how you are going to approach it?"

"The people on the financial side seem to be united in opposition. Can we count on you to back our proposal?"

In every work environment, there are times when you need the support of others, or they need your support, in order to reach goals. Your connections with others, your ability to organize a lobby, your vote, your voice in a meeting, and your diplomacy are all resources you can exchange.

We see these kinds of exchanges all the time in the legislative process. Congresswoman X supports Congressman Y's bill in exchange for Y's vote on her home state's pet project. The same kinds of exchanges can be made equitably and profitably in your workplace. They may apply to colleagues more than to subordinates, but they can nonetheless help you create the kind of change you want.

Equipment, Supplies, and Space

Kathy looks at you over the top of her half-frame glasses and leans in closer. Her voice drops a register, a sure sign she's not in your office for her own entertainment. "I've spent the last morning I ever care to spend unjamming that archaic copier," she hisses through her teeth. "That machine has cost me time, three fingernails, and it's threatening my sanity. Now, are you going to push through my request for a new machine, or should I have the break room insulated for primal scream therapy?"

As a manager, you may control office, or department, budgets that can contribute to improved working conditions for your employees. Being able to provide new furniture, equipment, or an occasional social event is a resource sometimes overlooked. Even if you can't directly provide these things, your ability to make requests to those who can, your ability to go to bat for your employees on these requests, can be a resource they will be willing to trade for.

Frequently, when employees make these kinds of requests, they will tell you they desperately need the things they are asking for. Faced with this kind of need, you may feel as if you are being cold and calculating when you offer to trade on it. But remember, asking for something of comparable value in return is merely reestablishing equity in the relationship. What you are doing is simply acknowledging their needs and then telling them your needs in return. They ask you to help them out; you ask them to help you out. These kinds of exchanges occur more or less automatically in good relationships. We describe the process as cooperation, mutual respect, or teamwork.

Based on Kathy's complaint about the copying machine, you propose, "I'll tell you what, Kathy. If you will get your people to complete all of their written job descriptions, and the procedures manuals, I'll go to the executive committee and fight to get the budget authorization for a new copier." Kathy agrees to your trade but as she leaves your office, she turns back to face you, her bulk filling the door frame.

"While you're at it, tell those people we need more room for the clerical staff. I've got the data entry clerks stacked up like cordwood in the back corner and secretaries sitting closer together than teenagers at a drive-in movie."

Here's another motivational resource at your disposal. If you have control over the amount, type, and configuration of space in your workplace, you may be able to make some very attractive offers in exchange for the behaviors you want.

Not all requests are made as directly as these and not all resources are identified as readily. Sometimes, and perhaps more often than not, subordinates tell you what you've got that they want indirectly, veiling their requests behind suggestive questions and comments. They might say something like, "Those people in purchasing could hold a barn dance in those offices, they've got so much room." Listen carefully to what they are saying and you may discover a wealth of resources you never knew existed.

Information

Woody leans against the credenza in your office, the picture of coolness, tossing a pencil into the air and catching it. "So, how did things go in Washington?" he asks nonchalantly. "You see anything of the new prototype engineering has cooked up?"

Conversational gambits? Hardly. These casual questions are usually indirect requests for the information you possess. Co-workers can benefit from knowing more about high-level company strategy, advance technical findings, restricted reports, or the inner workings of the organization. You may be able to use this information to create change, by offering it as part of an exchange.

You might say to Woody, "The meeting in Washington was really interesting. I'd love to tell you about it later. Tell you what. If you will get those reports corrected for me so that I can review them, I'll be happy to fill you in on it before you go home."

Informal Activities

Gene, who seems to have been hanging around a lot lately, catches up with you on your way to the employee garage. "Pat, when you installed that skylight in your bathroom, what kind of prep work did you have to do? You know, I've been thinking about a similar project at my house, and I was curious to know how you did it."

You offer to loan Gene the manual you used, but he turns you down. "Oh, you know, I read those books, but they just don't do it for me. I have trouble picturing what they are saying. I do so much better when I can see an actual example."

Just before you offer Gene the name of the building supply company you visited, the light bulb finally goes off. While Gene would probably be too embarrassed to admit it, what he really wants to do is come by your house. What he wants even more has nothing to do with your skylight. Gene wants a little of your time and attention off site.

Many employees value sharing informal activities with superiors because it gives them more insight into the people for whom they work and offers a chance to build friendships and coalitions. Informal activities such as office visits, shared meals, invitations to parties, and get-togethers at home are another cluster of resources you may want to use to create profitable and equitable exchanges.

Supervision

"I am so sick of having to make sure that everything we do here matches the directives from the home office," James complains to you one morning. "Would the world stop spinning if just once you didn't check to make sure we followed every directive to the letter?"

Your ability to control the amount of supervision an employee receives is another source of change incentives. James, and many other employees, feel more valued and trusted if they are allowed to work with a minimum amount of supervision. Your willingness to trim the amount of reporting, or allow some latitude in

compliance with often tedious bureaucratic requirements, could be a very attractive item of trade with
employees.

All you have to do to turn James's complaint into a
resource is to offer to change what he is complaining
about as part of a contingency. "Well, James, I know
how deadening it can be to be chained to all those
directives. I'll tell you what. You see that the next ten
print runs go out of here error-free, and I'd be willing
to consider how strictly I monitor all of your procedures."

Sally's gripe comes from the other direction.
"Couldn't you take ten minutes a week just to let me
know how I'm doing? It makes me nervous to work for
weeks without you seeing my work yourself."

Like Sally, some employees, particularly those new
to an organization, or working on new projects, value
frequent supervisory feedback on their work. By paying attention to their complaints or comments you can
determine which resource—more supervision or less—
is going to motivate which employee.

Sometimes you can also actually create resources
by oversupervising employees. When you're faced with
an employee who is performing below your expectations, increase the amount of supervision and scrutiny
this employee gets. At the very least, this will ensure
that his work will meet minimum standards. However,
you may also find that the close supervision will
prompt the employee to ask for less supervision. As
soon as that request is made, you're in a position to
make the changes you want.

Communication

"I feel like the proverbial mushroom around here. You never tell me anything."

"I was really embarrassed to find out at the supervisor's meeting that you were postponing implementation of the new software system. It makes me mad that you don't alert me to those decisions before telling the whole group."

"Do you mind looking at this report and telling me what you think? I'd really like your opinion before I present it."

Requests for inside information, advanced briefings on company business, or for your advice all suggest possible communication resources at your disposal.

Praise

"You never have anything nice to say about all the meeting arrangements I make for you."

"I wish the rest of the guys in my department recognized what a coup that was to get the Henderson account."

"You liked my report? So tell headquarters that, will you?"

"Can you write me a letter of recommendation?"

Words of praise are a great motivator for many employees. Recognition from you personally, praise before their peers, notice to their superiors, and congratulatory letters to them, or in their personnel file, are resources you possess in abundance. When people come to you with these requests, be prepared to give them what they want in exchange for what you want.

A manager with a reputation for being distant and

cold is sitting on a mountain of resources. His subordinates are probably so starved for a few kind words, that he could get them to agree to climb Mount Everest if he would agree to start saying, "Good job."

Unofficial Benefits

Bob's a nice guy whose performance in the collection department has been running poor-to-mediocre lately. You've discussed it with him, and he's said he'll work on it, but he's still running behind schedule on his required customer contacts. It's Monday morning, and he's coming into your office now.

"Hey, Roger, I've got to run a bunch of stuff off this weekend for my son's pack meeting. Do you mind if I come in on Sunday and use the computer and the copier?"

Bob is assuming that you'll automatically grant this request. Employees come to view the space, facilities, discounts, and supplies they enjoy at work as their own. Don't let them take those things for granted. Keep the decision-making control in your hands and make use of these unofficial benefits as trading assets.

Bob's request is the perfect opportunity to offer a trade to get the changes you want. Because employees take many of these resources for granted, it is sometimes necessary to amplify what those resources cost you. Taking the time to explain how much of your time and attention it will take helps to clarify the exchange being made.

"I'd be happy to write a memo authorizing that, but it will take me some time to compose, and then I'll have to see who I can get to type it. If you will make certain that you get through your call bin every day this

week and bring your 30-, 60-, and 90-day accounts up
to date, then I'll be happy to have it ready for you by
Friday.''

Your Personal Storehouse

You stop by Dan's desk, thinking you're going to talk
with him about speeding up the timetable on the Wel-
don contract, but you find him cradling his head in one
hand and holding a balled up piece of paper in the
other. Dan, it turns out, is in the midst of an ugly
dispute with his neighbor over their common property
line. "Geez, Harriet," he tells you. "I can't believe it's
come to this. The guy has filed a harassment suit
against me. It looks like I'm going to need a good
attorney and fast.''

You have resources outside the work environment,
culled from your personal relationships. You may have
connections with professionals through your health
club, friends in other businesses, or a nephew with a
truck you could borrow for the guy two offices down
who is moving next weekend. All are assets you can
draw on to get the changes you want.

You enthusiastically say, "Dan, there is a woman I
play racquetball with who is a great attorney. Tell you
what, why don't you finish that letter to our suppliers
that I asked you to write yesterday and bring it to my
office when you finish. I'll make some calls and find out
her office phone number and give it to you when you
bring me the letter.''

Third-Party Trades

There will be times when you are dying to make a trade with someone, but they never come to you for anything. You simply don't have anything that they want. A trade is still possible if you broaden your scope.

Suppose you really want accounting to give your salespeople an extra week to submit their travel vouchers. Accounting needs nothing from you. Accounting, however, would love to get its hands on a new software program, but purchasing is waiting to get a better buy.

It happens that purchasing wants a priority shipment from an office supply company with which you've had frequent friendly dealings. Here's your bargaining chip. When Jane from purchasing comes to you and asks you to talk to your contact at the supply company about their order, you might respond, "Jane, I'll be glad to help you out. I think I can get them to come through for you. Actually there's something you can do for me, too. Accounting requires that expense vouchers be turned in within five days of a sales trip and this is burdensome to my staff. I want accounting to allow ten days for vouchers on a three-month trial basis. If you'd talk to Clara in accounting about instituting this as a pilot project, I'd be happy to talk to my friends at AFC about getting your order rushed."

This bartering system, if used effectively, equitably, and profitably, will benefit all three parties. Accounting gets their software, purchasing gets its supplies in a hurry, and you get the change you want.

Money, Money, Money

When most people think of resources that other people want, all they think of are financial rewards. Notice that pay and salary haven't been included on the list of resources reviewed so far. Money is definitely a high-value resource to people, and can be an effective incentive. If you control how much your employees get paid, you have a tremendous resource at your disposal.

Many of us have only very limited control over basic salary, however. We may be able to recommend raises, but the final decision is always made in consideration of job grade, experience, etc. But don't despair. In fact, you may have control over some dollars you could use as incentives.

Orson is glumly loading up the serrating machine when you cross the floor. You ask him why he's got such a sour face, and he shakes his head and shuts down his machine for a minute.

"We just took my boy Jimmy into the orthodontist. You got any idea how much braces cost? They're not covered on the dental plan, either. I don't know how I can afford it on my hourly."

You can't change Orson's hourly wage rate, but if Orson needs money for braces, maybe you could create some overtime work for him. If a salesperson wants more money, maybe you could offer a special, one-time cash bonus in exchange for him developing a sales-training program for new hires. Perhaps an employee is willing to exchange higher production quota, or improved budget control, for a job with special benefits attached. Money doesn't come only in paychecks, and you may have some of these options available.

Advancement

You offer Bill the chance to make some extra money by working overtime if he will teach the two new guys on his shift how to operate the new equipment. As you conclude this exchange, he tells you something else that has been on his mind.

"I'm aiming for the assistant manager's position, but what I really need is some strong backing. I know I've got the background and skill for the job."

You don't have to guarantee him the job just because he asked, but you could set out productivity goals for Bill and his group.

"Bill, if you can get your group to consistently achieve that level of output, then I'd be willing to seriously consider you as a candidate for the assistant manager position."

Promotions should clearly be earned, not given away because of years of service or years of whining about wanting a promotion. In this example, Bill is working to earn the right to be given serious consideration for the opening.

You may not have total control over who gets promoted or gets transferred to your company's most desirable locations, but you may have some degree of control over your subordinates' chances for promotion. Your commendations for excellent performance, your written reviews and verbal comments to superiors, and your ability to recommend employees for promotion are all resources you can tap.

Personnel, Budget, and Benefits

These are key motivational resources usually controlled by upper management. You're in a very powerful position if you decide on the number of employees hired, who is hired, who is fired, who gets a full-time position, who works as a temporary employee, and which jobs get reclassified and upgraded.

You may also control departmental budgets. How much money a department gets, how accountable managers are for its use, what they must accomplish with that money, and how it is apportioned, may all be at your discretion. Here a trade may be for a department's performance as a whole: "If your group successfully implements the entire Total Quality Plan by the end of the fiscal year, with no decrease in productivity, then I'll give you the 15-percent budget increase you are requesting."

Salary levels, management flexibility in assigning wages, bonuses, merit increases, and an entire host of financial benefits may be at your disposal. You may have the ability to decide what kind of health-care coverage your employees receive, what level of life insurance you'll provide, and what kinds of investment opportunities you'll make available to those who work for you. Every one of these has great potential for use in trading and in shaping the behavior of those who work with and for you.

When You Still Can't Think of Anything

If you still haven't identified the resources you possess that will motivate certain employees, you can always ask:

"Is there anything that I could do to make your job easier?"

"Can you think of anything that would make this a more pleasant place for you to work?"

This questioning can be done more formally as a part of a performance appraisal or a discussion of goals. Meeting individually with subordinates, peers, and even superiors to find out where they are heading and what things they want to achieve will often stimulate you to think of ways you could help them achieve their goals. As they itemize their desires, they are also listing your potential resources.

Often you can't predict what people consider a reward, and you can only learn by asking. Just letting an employee determine which jobs he does, or the order in which he does them, may sometimes be a reward. Don't be afraid to ask people what you could do for them.

Cataloging Your Resources

As you prepare to trade for the changes you want, a catalog of your hidden motivational resources can be an exceptionally useful tool. Spend a week simply jotting down all of the requests people make of you, regardless of how minor or outrageous they may seem. If a request from one person brings to mind a request made in the past by someone else, add it to your list. By the end of that week, you'll be surprised at the length of your list.

Spend some time examining your important workplace relationships. Does Peg usually ask you to change her work schedule? Is Jack always coming to you and asking for overtime? What about your supervisor? Does she frequently ask for your technical expertise?

Identifying the matches between your co-worker's needs and your resources you will put you in a position to start making the trades that will produce the changes you want.

You've probably been asked for and given away so many of these things so often that you've never stopped to think of them as resources. Take the time to identify the many assets over which you have discretionary control. Potentially all of these could be used to make trades for the kinds of changes you are seeking. Just because you have given them away freely in the past doesn't mean you have to continue the giveaway program. You can change your behavior, too.

Of course, you can continue to give resources away for free if you want to. Bear in mind, however, that when you are dealing with a resistor, you may be giving away your best chance to create the kinds of change you want. If you begin to spend these riches wisely by using them to make equitable exchanges in the form of contingencies, you'll find that you can create changes much more readily.

CHAPTER SIX

A Field Guide to Resistance Tactics

You make a simple request, but instead of immediate action, you get one of these responses:

"That will never work. We tried it before. Your approach is way off target."

"After all we've been through together, I can't believe you'd ask me to do this. I thought you were my friend. What a fool I've been."

"Do you have to use that tone of voice with me?"

"Why do you want to initiate this plan in the Southeast? And why wait until third quarter to do it?"

"I'll be happy to give it a try. I'm not sure I can pull it off, but I'll give it my best shot."

"I can't do that now. I've got the month-end reports to finish, Mia is out sick, and the computer just went down."

"How can you ask me to do that? I can't believe you're being so insensitive."

"I've been with this company for twenty-eight years and we've always done it this way. It's just too late in the game to ask me to change now."

You may get silence, accompanied by a slack-mouthed, blank-eyed stare. Or, you may hear what you think you wanted to hear:

"No problem. I promise I'll get right on it."

All of these responses—including the deceptively promising yes—are tactics resistors use to avoid changing. Instead of action, you're getting a barrage of rhetoric, endless emotional outbursts, questions, and non-verbal behavior that demands your attention and draws you away from your real goal of producing change.

Some of these resistance devices are so subtle and convincing that it may take years before you figure out what is really happening. Once you learn to identify these tactics, however, you can learn to avoid them. The first step is to understand that all of the tactics are designed to achieve one of four broad strategic goals: distraction; buying time; wearing you down; and pseudo-agreement. Each of the four strategies creates a different trap to ensnare you. By quickly recognizing resistance for what it is, you can side-step getting caught.

DISTRACTIONS

The magician dramatically raises the fluttering pigeon high in his left hand. While all eyes watch the bird, he deftly rearranges the cards with his right hand. Resistors, too, create variations of this time-honored ploy—distraction. The resistor introduces a diversion to shift

the discussion away from the change you are requesting. Almost any alternative topic will do as long as it
will engage your attention. In the following instances,
you will see the element of distraction become bla-
tantly clear.

A Show of Emotion

You see a work group that's lagging behind all the
others and decide on a corrective plan of action. Hoping to avoid a group confrontation, you decide to meet
privately with each team member so you can suggest
the changes to each of them individually.

You outline your plan for change to Talia. She juts
out her chin and squints her eyes in a clear show of
anger. Next you meet with Dabny. He responds with
an open mouth and wounded puppy eyes. Figuring the
third time is a charm, you make your request of Liz.
Liz responds by fumbling through her pockets for a
handkerchief to mop up the coming tears.

As you restate your request, your employees may
back up their nonverbal reactions with words.

"I'm shocked."

"I'm so stunned, I don't know what to say."

"I can't believe you're asking me to do this."

If you respond to these emotional displays in the
usual way by answering anger with anger, sadness with
compassion, and tears with comforting words, you will
fall right into the resistors' trap.

These emotional pyrotechnics effectively distract
you from the topic of change and launch you into a
discussion of the resistor's emotions. Effectively
played, a show of emotions is sufficiently dramatic to
upstage your request for change. Instead of concentra-

ting on the change you want to make, your time and energy will be directed to the other person's feelings.

These emotional displays will certainly appear to be authentic. No resistance tactic is effective without at least a semblance of sincerity. And they may, in fact, be authentic. People do get angry and hurt. Whether those displayed feelings are real, deliberate, or planned is hard to determine, but their practical effect is clear. The resistors rearrange the agenda so that you deal with their emotions, and the change you want is put on hold.

Criticizing Your Methods

Once again you state your proposal for change, but what you hear is:

"Why do you always use such a superior tone of voice with me?"

"Why do you have to raise your voice every time you want something?"

"What do you mean, I **never** get reports in on time?"

This resistance tactic switches the focus away from *what* you said and on to *how* you said it. The resistor ignores the content of your request and gets you to focus on how you've communicated your request. If your voice isn't a problem, your timing could be.

"I just got in, and I'm not up to speed yet. Do we have to talk about this now?"

"Look, it's almost six and I'm exhausted. Why bring this up now?"

"Hey, it's Friday afternoon. Are you trying to ruin my weekend?"

"I'm sorry, but I'm under a lot of strain at home. Can't this wait for another day?"

Notice the punctuation here. Everything ends in a question mark—for good reason. By asking a question, the resistor draws you into providing an answer and away from concentrating on your request.

One interesting variation switches the topic to the medium of your communication.

"What's the idea of sending me a written memo on a matter like this? With something this sensitive, I expect you to come to me in person."

So, the next time a similar matter comes up, you go to him in person, and what does he say?

"Look, I need something in writing for a matter that is this sensitive."

It's always possible to find fault with how someone is making a request, so criticizing the method provides an easy way for the resistor to switch the focus of discussion and avoid change.

Name-Calling

You tell an employee that you're unhappy with some aspect of his performance and ask him to make a change.

"Everything has to be your way. Can't you ever let me do something my way? Isn't that what you hired me for?"

"You don't think my work is up to par? With all of the pressure I've been under? Don't you think you're being unfair?"

"Why are you picking on me? Nobody else has been asked to take on this much work."

When faced with these indictments of our good name, most of us aid and abet the resistor by defending ourselves. We switch our conversation away from the change request over to defending against the attack upon our character. Score one for the resistor.

In the ensuing confrontation, the resistor's face may appear angry, but inside he's smiling. The moment you start to defend yourself, he knows that he has distracted you from pressuring him to change. Mission accomplished.

"I Thought You Were My Friend."

You approach a trusted and valued employee, co-worker, or supervisor with your request for a change, and instead of agreement, you hear one of these responses:

"After all the times I've saved your neck, now you do this to me?"

"Jack, you said you were my friend, and I believed you. This makes it clear you never did think of me as a friend. Obviously, the company comes first with you, and I don't even rate a hearing."

"You know, Faye, I completely trusted you to protect my interests. I mean, after all we've been through together, I can't believe you'd turn on me like this. What a fool I've been."

"My own brother does this to me? Dad must be crying in his grave."

The use of this resistance tactic reaches epidemic proportions in both the workplace and at home. It switches the topic of discussion from your proposal to the broader canvas of your whole relationship with the person you're asking to make a change.

The intimation is that, because you share a special bond of friendship with a person, you're taking unfair advantage and betraying their trust if you ask them to make this change. If you let them, these resistors will switch the topic of discussion from your change request to your failure to act like a loving friend "after all these years."

Trying to convince the person that you do, in fact, like or love them only leads to a long-winded, futile argument. The concepts of friendship, love, trust, and respect are so general that they are open to broad interpretation. The altitude of such discussion quickly rises to about 40,000 feet and pulls you with it up, up, and away from your request for change.

According to them, the only way you can prove beyond doubt that you are their true friend, worthy of their trust, and sincerely appreciative of all they've done for you is to immediately withdraw your request. That is the resistor's real goal because it guarantees things will stay just the way they are.

Red Herrings

In past centuries, English farmers used to employ their own method of distraction. They'd drag smelly fish—red herrings—around the edges of their fields. Hunting dogs were thrown off the scent of the prey, and the farmers' crops were then left untrampled by the gentry on horseback. The technique was so effective that modern workers have adapted it for use in the contemporary business world.

You call Mel in for a meeting to discuss his sales reports. He doesn't even sit down before he starts telling you about the new prospects he's uncovered in a new market segment. He starts feeding you projected sales figures. You admit they sound great. He's got you hooked and now he starts tugging on the line.

How would you approach this new market? Should more salespeople be brought into the picture now or should they run some projections before doing that? If just the prospects he's already identified pan out, can you imagine what annual sales would be?

Any number of topics would suit Mel's purpose of diversion, but each must have two elements. It must enable him to sound authentically involved, and the topic must be sufficiently complicated to require extended discussion. If both elements are present, then even a rather straightforward switch will distract you. Mel resists by leading you away from the topic of his performance before you even have a chance to bring it up.

Subordinates aren't the only ones adept at using birdies and red herrings. Bosses and others in positions of authority can do so even when you've scheduled a meeting to make a specific proposal. Has this ever happened to you?

As soon as you've entered the superior's sanctum, he begins to draw you into his confidence.

"I just got some new information from headquarters this morning I haven't had a chance to discuss with anyone. You're an astute judge of these things. Do you mind if I bounce some of this off of you, so I can get a better reading on it?"

Thinking you're about to get the inside scoop—which can be a valuable resource—you give him the floor. He then launches into a convoluted discussion of general topics that doesn't include anything particularly useful and may actually be old news. He solicits your opinion often enough to keep the discussion going, and that's the point. His topic eats up time until his next scheduled appointment, and he's safely shuffled you out the door before you even have a chance of introducing your proposal.

Supervisors can get even more mileage out of this tactic if their topic includes a reference to your "future with the firm."

"We're going to be rattling some cages around here, making some big changes. There are a couple of people we're going to be watching very carefully, people we know are real team players. Of course, I'm not at liberty to say much more, but I can say that one or two people are going to be moving up the ladder two or three rungs at a time pretty soon. Now, what was it you wanted to discuss?"

How nervy are you? If your next promotion is at least implicitly on the line here, are you going to rock the boat by asking your boss to change his ways? By dropping hints about future benefits for good little team players, he can effectively deflect you even at your most assertive.

BUYING TIME

The clock keeps running as you discuss these extraneous topics. The resistor keeps adding items to the agenda, and pretty soon there is no time left for your request. Perhaps there will be time tomorrow, next week, or at the planning meeting next quarter. In the meantime, however, because the discussion of your request never comes to a conclusion, the resistor doesn't have to change. Here are some of the tactics that are frequently used to waste time and delay change.

Instrumental Ignorance

You introduce your proposal and your employee's face reflects bewilderment. "Let me see if I understand you," he says, and then gives you a completely inaccurate summary of what you just said.

You know you can make this understandable, so you explain the proposal again. Now he's even more confused. He apologizes for his slow wit, and asks if you'd mind explaining just one more time. You think of yourself as a clear communicator and have the patience of a saint, so you describe the request once more. The puzzled look on your employee's face remains.

The problem here isn't a lack of communication. It's a lack of incentive. This employee can't understand what you're asking him to do because it's not in his self-interest to understand. If he understood, then he'd have to do what you want. If he can convince you he doesn't understand your proposal, he won't have to comply with it.

Sometimes, just as you consider giving up, the other person will toss you a crumb. The light of understanding dawns upon his or her face. Suddenly, one element of your proposal becomes clear. This keeps you in the game, and you continue with your explanations. Further information, of course, may again cloud the understanding.

Since you're ever hopeful, you continue to try to explain. When superiors use this tactic they may suggest you run it by them again in a few weeks, using more graphics or maybe a video. That will make all the difference in the world. Right.

Before you conclude that you're dealing with people with diminished mental capacities, take a look at what these apparently slow-witted parties have achieved. When you finally storm away in anger and disgust, the resistor is free to lean back and enjoy his victory. Who's slow-witted here?

If you think about it, deliberate misunderstanding has an honored position outside the workplace, too. In marriages, both partners play the game. He doesn't understand why she doesn't understand why he needs nights out with the boys. Your six-year-old doesn't understand why she has to make her bed in the morning when she is only to going to get back into it at night. Generations of teenagers have failed to see the value of a curfew.

When subordinates keep misunderstanding, you may reach your limit and explode:

"I don't care whether or not you understand. Just do what I'm telling you to do." The skilled resistor has a ready comeback for such authoritarian outbursts. "Oh, so I'm not supposed to think. Just do whatever you order me to do. I suppose it's somehow my fault you can't explain what you want in simple language. It's always my fault. And you're the one who is always talking about clear communication." Gotcha.

Why? Why? Why?

In your new position as national marketing director, you have never before addressed all of the district sales managers. Adding to your anxiety is the fact that you are laying out a comprehensive new marketing program. So far the presentation has gone flawlessly and the smiles on the sales managers' faces in the audience suggest that they like your proposal. As you conclude, a hand goes up and you hear:

"This sounds great," Sue, from the Southwest,

says with enthusiasm, "but I'm confused about one small point. Do you mind if I ask a question?"

You don't want to dampen her enthusiasm, especially since it sounds as if she's on your side, so of course you say yes.

"Why do you want to initiate a completely new marketing plan?" She asks, earnest sincerity written all over her face.

You explain, and she responds.

"Please don't get me wrong, I really like your plan, but I don't understand why you want to do this now rather than waiting till spring?" You explain further, hoping to clarify matters.

"Okay, but why are we initiating it in Cary's region instead of Leslie's?"

You're running out of time, but Sue's interest deserves your attention, so you elaborate.

Next she asks, "I hate to persist in this, but I really want to understand your thinking. Don't you think we should introduce the change using just one or two products at a time rather than risk the whole line?"

The earnest concern behind this resistance tactic has helped make it one of the all-time favorites. It's pretty hard to fault an employee when all she is doing is seeking more information.

Is that all she's doing? Sue's apparently innocent questions have forestalled any chance of initiating the new plan, they've eaten up your time, and they've consumed a whole lot of energy. And it's not over. Subsequent sessions with Sue will probably prompt more questions. She may argue details with you, or she may push you to expand the subject. Her goal is not so much to understand, but to block your new proposal because it would disrupt the comfortable niche she has built for herself.

Your responses to Sue's questions, given as earnestly as they were asked, have led you off track, delayed change, and worn you down. That's why this tactic works so well.

Complicating the Issue

A resistor can take your simple request for change and blow it up into an impossibly complex and time-consuming proposition.

"Before we do anything, I think we ought to consider this from a historical perspective. Why don't we bring Dustin in on this? He's been here for three decades and may be able to offer some insight. And Ted worked on a similar project during the Kennedy administration. Let's set another meeting with them and look at this thing from a broader point of view."

"I think maybe it would be more beneficial to take a systems approach to this proposal. Have you considered all the ramifications this is going to have? Don't get me wrong, I like the idea. I just feel we ought to study this in detail before implementation."

The more topics and people that are included, the less likely it is that you'll get what you want. Your request gets so encumbered with other ideas and the whole mess becomes an omnibus bill. Eventually, it gets so complicated that you decide it's just not worth the time and energy to pursue it. Score a big one for the resistor.

Excuses

Your proposal for a change may draw one of these responses:

"You know, Spike, if we had better equipment, I wouldn't be behind in the first place."

"This is the way we have always done it."

"I know I haven't been meeting quotas, but the kids have been sick and it really puts me under a lot of stress."

"So many things are in flux right now, I just can't keep track of them all. Please don't add even more."

The equipment is old, and it breaks. It's new, and it's got kinks. There are too many engineers and not enough support staff, or too few engineers and too many staffers. Perhaps current events have people too depressed to do anything, or too excited to concentrate. There is always a good excuse.

You can undoubtedly add to the list from your experience. People are very creative at identifying extenuating circumstances that explain why they can't go along with your request. They keep inventing them until you get completely sidetracked, or exhausted, and give up even asking.

"So What You're Saying Is . . ."

You carefully state your request for a change in procedures and get a reinterpretation that leaves your head reeling.

"So what you're really saying is that you never want me to make any decisions. You want me to check with you before I so much as order new pencils. Well, I don't think that's fair at all. After all, I'm an adult, and if you can't trust me to make those kind of decisions on my own, well, I don't know what I'm doing here."

Your request has been stretched beyond recognition, and bears only the slightest resemblance to what you actually said. Now you must take time to reexplain exactly what you meant.

The domestic equivalent of this technique is to take your request and use it to redefine your feelings.

"So what you're saying is that you don't trust me enough to do this alone? Well, obviously, if you don't trust me, you certainly can't respect me and how can you love anyone you don't trust and respect?"

Warning signals should go off the moment you hear the phrase, "So, what you are saying is . . ."

WEARING YOU DOWN

A third group of resistance tactics goes beyond distraction and wasting time. These tactics wear you down by turning every request into a burden not worth bearing. Whether they trap you in a heated battle, or sink you in a rhetorical swamp, these tactics convince you to give up any effort to make a change and just leave things the way they are.

Combative Wordfare

You outline your expectations for change, and the other person rapidly fires off a list of all the things wrong with it. If you try to defend your position, the battle is engaged, and the resistor has already won the war.

You may think that you can use logic, reason, evidence, and experience to convince the resistor of the correctness of your request, but no explanation is going to get him to agree with you. If he agrees with you, he'll have to change, and it's his goal to avoid change.

Initially, the argument may be civil and calm. But, as each of your points is contradicted or dismissed, your emotions will begin to rise. What begins as a logical discussion soon turns into a shouting match. That is just what the resistor is aiming for.

Once you're good and hot, the resistor may switch to the role of cool diplomat.

"Look, it's clear we're not getting anywhere. Let's just call it quits for now. We can come back to this in a few days when you've calmed down."

You may welcome the cessation of hostilities and agree. If you do, you are allowing the resistor to further postpone having to change.

The resistor may also use the argument as a base from which to launch an attack on your management style.

"It's no use talking to you because it ends up in a fight every time. You walk around preaching about open communication and yet every discussion with you turns into an argument that doesn't accomplish a thing."

With this, he blocks your request for change by effectively cutting off any further discussion and simultaneously slings some mud in your direction. How much more of this do you want to take? The resistor will keep at it until he wears you down.

Trivialization

Your request for change is met with a condescending smirk and a terse acknowledgment:

"I appreciate your concern, but I think you're losing sight of the big picture here. We're working on some really dynamic plans in my department, and I really think we're better off spending our time on those than on worrying about these details. I mean, what's more important here?"

"Honestly, I'm managing a two-million-dollar purchasing budget and you want me to get competitive bids for these things? Don't you think that's being just a little nit-picky?"

"You can't see the forest for the trees. What's important here is the big picture, not these minor details. We can take care of those small details later."

This tactic takes your request and frames it in the grand scheme of things where it becomes petty and insignificant. The goal is to make your request seem trivial, so that both you and the resistor can overlook it and move on to more "important" things.

Old Dogs, Old Tricks

You've been in your new position for a month now, and feel the time is right to start introducing some of the innovative management techniques you learned in your former position. Full of enthusiasm, you present the strategies to your branch manager, Burt. He listens closely, but once you've made your request, he just smiles and shakes his head.

"You don't really expect me to start that now, after all these years, do you? I've run my staff meetings the same way for years, and my way has been pretty effective. You can't expect me to learn this new participative management stuff at this late date."

Or, you propose a change to your boss, and you get the second verse:

"I've been with this company for twenty-eight years now. I'm not about to change my stripes now. You're asking me to alter a pattern I've followed for so long, it's part of my personality. I'd like to accommodate you, but it just can't be done."

A variation on this theme is the notion that people just are the way they are.

"You knew when you hired me I was an introvert. You can't expect me to start playing showman now. I'm just not like that."

"I can't help it if all those statistical reports aren't done. I'm a conceptualizer, a visionary, not a detail-oriented number cruncher."

All of these responses are variations on the old saying, "You can't teach an old dog new tricks." This tactic tries to draw you away from your request for change by convincing you that you're asking for the impossible. People, like old dogs, are supposedly unchangeable. Unfortunately, we go along with such conclusions because traditional psychology tells us to do so.

Reluctant Acceptance

You know that Graham hates to do detailed paperwork, and so you have postponed asking him to go back through the files to recalculate each customer's debt ratio using the new formula. Your boss keeps asking for the figures, though, so you finally go to Graham and spell out what you want him to do.

"Okay," he sighs in response. "If that's what you want. I'll dredge up all those past accounts and go through them with a fine-tooth comb."

While saying these apparently agreeable words,

Graham heaves a weary sigh, shakes his head no, avoids eye contact, and raises his arms in surrender.

You sense that reluctant yes means no, so you ask Graham if he has a problem with your request. That question is just the one he wanted you to ask. That was the goal of his sigh and long face. By asking if he has a problem, you give him permission to express all his doubts about your idea.

He has distracted you. Now, you'll spend time explaining, and he'll just keep disagreeing or not understanding. Eventually, you'll just give up and drop the subject and the resistor won't have to do what you want.

Defiant Acceptance

Everybody thought that Ted would get the job of department head, but instead they hired you from outside the company. It's day one and the tension is thick. As you meet with the department members to outline the duties you want them to assume, each one reacts with the same emotional tone.

"If that's what I have to do to keep my job, I guess that's what I'll do."

"Sure, I'll add an extra ten hours a week to my work load."

"Are you ordering me to do this?"

All these responses are delivered in a tightly controlled voice with the anger behind them only thinly disguised. You can't help but recognize the defiance in these reactions, but if follow your first impulse and ask what's wrong, you'll get a cascade of hostility. Such overwhelming adversity is enough to get most of us to back down from our requests by labeling them as only tentative suggestions.

Catatonia

Sitting across from you is an employee staring at you with dead eyes and a slack mouth. He says nothing, but you can sense contempt for you and your request. You keep restating your proposal in what you hope are more palatable terms. When you're finally talked out, he'll say something like this:

"Are you done?"

"Can I go now?"

This is catatonia, a stratagem mastered by six-year-olds and practiced until the grave. Turnips are more animated than people using this tactic.

The catatonic says virtually nothing and, sensing his seething disagreement, you decide to drop the subject. You are tired of doing battle, so you stop asking.

PSEUDO-AGREEMENT

Most discouraging of all resistance tactics are the ones which give you the feeling of victory. You walk away from the encounter with a sense of accomplishment and heightened confidence in your own management skill. All too soon, you are brought back down to reality when you learn that your communication skills produced only agreeable words, not real action.

Promises

As you state your request, the employee looks interested, nods agreement as you outline your proposal, and smiles encouragingly. Then he or she delivers the response you've been longing to hear:

"Sure, Patrick, I promise to get right on it."

"No problem. I give you my word. I'll take care of it."

How is this different from true agreement? The difference lies in the subsequent actions—or lack thereof. When you don't get the report, or the increase in production numbers, or the new accounting system, you return to the person who so cheerfully gave you a yes.

Now comes act two. These resistors begin to ask questions, show emotion, stare at you blankly, pretend ignorance, or make excuses for their noncompliance. Their promises say yes, yes, yes, but their inaction tells you that the real answer was no, no, no.

Ambiguous Language

You read a great article that describes some new ways to more efficiently organize the flow of work. You make copies of the article and eagerly give one to your three co-workers. As Jason accepts the article, he says, "Sure, sounds interesting, I'll give it a try." Sally also sounds intrigued, "I think this is do-able. Let me think about it."

The resistor doesn't promise to actually do what you want he only says he will "try" or "think about" your request. You'll discover this for yourself when you return two weeks later to ask about the new approach he said he would take. He quickly corrects you, "I said I'd try, and I did try. It just didn't work as well as the old way, so I just stayed with what worked."

The pleasing sound of ambiguous language gives you the false sense that you got what you wanted. An

145

amazing number of people are willing to try; a rare few actually deliver. Eventually we learn that the pseudo-agreement of ambiguous language means just one thing. The job won't get done.

Six Simple Steps for Getting Results

CHAPTER SEVEN

Laying the Groundwork

The Six-Step Process is a quick and simple method for managing resistance in the workplace. The process was developed over years of trial-and-error experience, and has been refined to enable you to handle even the most difficult cases. Thousands of people, in countless seminars and training sessions, have learned how to follow these six easy steps to get the changes they want, and with a little practice you'll have the same success. Armed with these concrete tools, you'll have the confidence and ability to solve your most troublesome people problems, and you'll do it with a minimum of stress and turmoil.

STEP 1: SETTING THE CONTEXT

Most of our encounters with resistors are doomed to failure before the meeting even begins. As soon as you suggest to Rick, your administrative assistant, that you meet to revisit an unpleasant issue, you can sense his hypervigilance. You can see in his nonverbal behavior that alarm systems are going off in his head. His mouth may twitch nervously, his eyes will look at anything but you, he may inexplicably start coughing or scratching his head.

The source of his fear is very specific: it results from his anticipation of the possible unpleasant consequences of this meeting. There are three primary negative consequences most people anticipate, which cause them to react defensively to your request.

First, resistors defend against criticism. They are prepared to fight if you suggest they are wrong, incompetent, or not performing properly. They must rebut your criticism because if you make those criticisms stick, that could lead to another set of more negative consequences.

Second, resistors defend against demotions. They anticipate they'll suffer a reduction of benefits, a reduction of responsibility, or possibly even lose their jobs.

Finally, resistors defend against inequity. They anticipate that they are going to be asked to do something that is going to cost them a great deal and for which they'll get little in return.

The first step in the Six-Step Process is designed to help you set up your meeting with the resistor without provoking these three alarms. By reducing the resistor's fear and defensiveness, you can improve your own chances for success.

Imagine that you have scheduled a meeting with Rick, an older employee who's been with the company a lot longer than you have. He's had his territory staked out long before you even joined the firm, and you've seen him bare his claws when anyone steps over his boundaries.

When Rick shows up at your office at the appointed time, his stern face sends a message before his mouth starts moving. Anticipating his demeanor, you'll probably try to look even tougher than he does.

Proving that you are bigger, stronger, or more powerful than Rick is not your goal. You're falling for his gambit of making this an emotionally unpleasant encounter. You are in control here, and you want this to be civil and positive.

Try a new approach. Instead of being severe, be pleasant and constructive.

1. Express sincere praise. When Rick comes in with his scowl, greet him with a smile. Get out from behind your desk cum barricade, walk to meet him, and offer him a warm handshake. Thank him for coming and invite him to take a seat.

Once you're both comfortable, take a minute to express sincere praise about one or two recent things Rick has done that you appreciated. Make certain your praise is truthful, realistic, and specific.

You don't have to personally like Rick to express this praise. You are complimenting him on specific things he has accomplished; you are not complimenting him on the sum total of his work performance, or his character. By praising particular accomplishments, you will be letting him know that you do not totally dislike him.

Your words and actions should communicate that you value the person's contribution. Whatever language you use, you want to deliver a message of acceptance. You also want to address problems quickly when they are still small and manageable. Many of us, fearing a long unpleasant encounter, postpone dealing with problems until we're ready to fire, or kill, someone. By tackling problems in small steps, as soon as they become apparent, you can make your encounters short, sweet, and to the point.

Your sincere praise turns off one of the resistor's inner alarms by reducing his need to defend against criticism. You may even see the results of your positive remarks, as the resistor begins relaxing his facial expression.

If you doubt the effectiveness of doing this, watch how you behave when you have to criticize a close friend. The first thing most of us do is to reassure our friend of our positive feelings and admiration.

"Look, Isaac, you know I value you as a friend and that I really admire the way you've been able to turn around your department."

Praise doesn't have to be reserved for friends. It can be just as effectively used with people who view you as an adversary. Try it five or six times.

2. Reaffirm the relationship. By reaffirming the future of your relationship with the other person, you eradicate his fear that you are about to terminate him, or reduce his responsibilities. You eliminate the second type of negative outcome the resistor thinks he has to defend against.

After your words of praise, you might say: "Rick, we've got some projects coming up next quarter where your experience and training will really be important to us. None of the plans are finalized yet, but it looks like you'll have a chance to show your stuff and make a contribution to the success of those projects."

The message you're delivering here is that Rick has a future with you, and your company. He's not about to be demoted or fired. As you talk about including him in future projects, Rick will read between the lines, and you'll see his defenses come down further as he visibly relaxes even more.

Some people try to send this reaffirming message with words such as, "Look, I'm not planning to fire you, but . . ." These words are a potential threat and usually arouse defensiveness rather than allaying it. Keep the discussion positive by alluding to future opportunities.

Again, consider the way you talk to your friends. One of the first things you do is reaffirm the future of the relationship.

"Issac, we've been good friends for six years and I look forward to our friendship growing in the years to come."

Again, you can use language that is comfortable for you, so long as it conveys the message that the problem you are about to discuss is not so serious that it threatens to jeopardize the whole relationship.

3. Keep your requests small. The last source of fear, the final negative consequence people defend against, is a request that will require them to make large costly changes.

You're not going to ask for huge changes, however. You're not going to make a major demand. You're going to create change one small step at a time, keeping resistance to a minimum. Going slowly, step-by-step, will produce less resistance and more change.

4. Express confidence in agreement. Your request for one small change can be blended into a single sentence that also expresses your confidence that the other person will agree with your request.

"Rick, there's one small thing I'd like to discuss with you, and I'm confident we can agree on it quickly."

"There's just one small thing we need to clarify and I'm sure we can resolve it quickly."

"There's just one minor detail we need to clear up, and I'm certain we can reach a mutually acceptable understanding on it."

You can state your request with confidence because you have good reason to believe that the change will be agreed to readily. You've waited until you have something the other person really wants, and you're about to propose an equitable trade that will enable him to get what he wants. Express that confidence in your words, tone of voice, and body language.

Acting uncertain will send the wrong signal to the resistor. Any wariness in making the request will suggest that, if the resistor puts up a big enough battle, you will probably back down.

Because we lack effective tools for producing change, and because we usually make requests at the worst possible time, we often begin these discussions by saying, "There's something I've been meaning to talk to you about. I know this is going to upset you, but we've really got to clear this up, so just let me get it out and then you can speak your piece."

This is an open invitation to resistance. You've told the other person you expect them to put up a battle and, with your encouragement, he'll promptly live up to your expectations.

People fall into this bumbling routine as a plea for sympathy and nonbelligerence. Most resistors accurately perceive the lack of confidence as a sign of weakness, which encourages them to resist even more forcefully. Practice what you are going to say, so that you can speak clearly and confidently.

Remember that you are holding something the resistor wants, and you are proposing a trade that is equitable and profitable. If he gets upset and says no to your request, you can always just say no to his.

5. Be brief. The resistor's strategy will be to drag up everything imaginable as a way of wearing you down. Your counter-strategy therefore should be to limit the meeting to a few minutes—five or ten maximum. Honestly tell him the exact time frame you've set for reaching an agreement.

"In fact, Rick, I'm so sure we can agree on this quickly that I've scheduled a conference in five minutes at 2:15. That should be enough time."

If you've taken two minutes to praise Rick, you might now look at your watch and recount, ". . . Make that three minutes. That should still be plenty of time. Why don't we get right to it? Here's what I propose."

Regardless of the language you use, convey a precise deadline. Checking your watch reinforces the message. Alluding to the specific activity you have to begin when the meeting is over also makes it easier to enforce the deadline. If you don't have anything you absolutely have to do, it might be worthwhile to invent something—a meeting you must attend, or a call you must make. You want to keep this meeting brief. Physically moving on to the next activity will help you end it.

Too often, we fall into the trap of imagining that any discussion with the resistor is going to take a long time. We know that is the way it has been in the past, so we assume it has to be like that in the future. It doesn't have to be. Anticipating that the encounter with the resistor will be unpleasant and time-consuming, we put it off as long as we can. When the problem can no longer be avoided, we block out an hour or two to do battle with the resistor.

Don't let the other person dictate the length of your encounter. Remember, you are in the high power position—you have something they want—so you get to decide matters of time.

Prior to meeting with the individual, decide how long *you want* to talk, not how long you're willing to talk. Five minutes is a reasonable amount of time to produce change in even the most difficult of resistors.

Setting a short deadline prior to a meeting is a good practice to use with both resistors and nonresistors. It focuses the discussion and leads to firm conclusions. If you want to spend more time, you can extend the time limit. This extension flatters the other person because it tells him that you value him, his ideas, and the project you are jointly discussing. Best of all, cutting the customary thirty-minute meetings to five or ten will save both of you a great deal of time.

STEP 2: STATING YOUR REQUEST

This is when you use the World's Most Persuasive Communication. In a matter of seconds, you can state the exchange designed to create change. This is the Change Contingency, and it contains both your request and the reward you're willing to give in exchange.

"Rick, if all of our pending files are updated by noon Friday, then you can leave work at 3:30 on Friday afternoon. Okay?"

That's it. Simply state the change contingency with a smile on your face and then say, "Okay?" "All right?" Agreed?" or "Do we have a deal?"

Say nothing more. You've made a reasonable proposal. Give the other person a chance to agree. If you smile and keep your mouth closed while you wait for agreement, you'll avoid the most colossal of blunders—continuing to talk. Too often we make the mistake of saying too much. Try to remember these DON'TS.

1. Don't give explanations. We delude ourselves by thinking that our good reasons are going to convince the resistor to do what we want. They aren't. If the resistor hasn't changed by this point, one more explanation is unlikely to do the trick. It's not in his self-interest to change. He thinks it's in his self-interest to resist. The persistent resistor will use your good reasons as ammunition with which to resist your request. He'll disagree with each of your reasons, distort them, misunderstand them, question them, and use them as bridges to all sorts of diversionary side trips that lead you both away from change. The more you talk, the easier it is for the resistor to resist. Simply be quiet.

At first it may seem a little awkward to remain silent after you state your request, so begin on a small scale. Start by being quiet for just three seconds. If you are an inveterate talker, these three seconds of silence can be an eternity. Try the three-second limit on five people. When you see that you can do this, and you see the startling results, move up to five seconds. Practice that with five more people. With practice, you'll soon be able to remain silent comfortably for ten seconds and then even longer.

This conversational vacuum will draw most people into giving you an answer. There will be holdouts, people who still say nothing. Give them fifteen seconds and then say, "You're smiling. Does that mean you agree?" Then with the same look of inquiring friendliness, smile at them for another fifteen seconds. They'll respond.

The resistor might surprise you completely and agree with your request. Given that you have what he wants, that you're offering an equitable trade, and that you've shut off the alarms against which he has to defend, this could very well happen. If he does agree immediately to the change, express your pleasure and move directly to Step 6, closure. If you don't receive a quick yes, then you move on to the next step in the process.

2. Don't delve into the past. The past is the resistor's turf because he can endlessly rewrite history to serve his purpose. If you bring up his past actions, prior policy, or previous discussions, you will be providing easy opportunities for him to waste time and avoid changing. Stay out of the past. Keep your request focused on the future and how you want him to behave in it.

3. Don't ask why. When someone repeatedly resists your requests for change, it is tempting to ask why.

"Rick, why do you keep avoiding updating the files? I don't understand. I've asked you five times, and you always have an excuse. What is going on?"

If you're honest with yourself, you'll probably admit that you're not really that interested in knowing why the person misbehaved. The critical tone of your questions usually implies that you don't want to listen to reasons. Your punitive manner suggests that no matter what the resistor says, there is no good reason for his action. By asking why, however, you've given him an opening for endless discussion and an easy way to avoid complying with your request.

STEP 3: EVALUATING THEIR RESPONSE

If the person says something other than yes to your request, you must carefully evaluate his response and decide if the objection is reasonable or resistant. This isn't always easy. You'll need to focus your attention solely on the resistor's reaction, and guard against prejudging what he says. It's easy to believe that if a person has repeatedly resisted your previous attempts to get him to change, he's likely to do it again. Give him the benefit of the doubt.

The guide to resistance tactics in Chapter 6 will help you determine whether the response is reasonable or resistant. Also, if you keep a list of the resistance tactics commonly used by your different work associates, you will have another reference to help you make this classification decision.

In almost every case, if the person says something that closely resembles the examples on these lists, you can be pretty sure it is resistance. There are two ambiguous cases, however. These are when the person gives you excuses for why he can't do what you want, and when he argues about the correctness of what you are requesting.

Usually when someone cites some extenuating circumstances for why he can't go along with your request, it is nothing more than an excuse, and you can circumvent it with the Bamboo Technique described in the next chapter.

Nevertheless, sometimes the person who always has an excuse comes up with a legitimate reason for why he cannot do as you ask. You need to carefully evaluate the plausibility of such statements, because sometimes they are reasonable. If you ask someone to move a heavy object, and he tells you he just pulled a muscle in his back, your call better be right. If you misjudge this as only an excuse to avoid work, you could face a disability claim as well as a lawsuit. Only you, with your detailed knowledge of the situation, can make this judgment.

In the same vein, arguments also require careful analysis. When someone openly criticizes or disagrees with your request, you may be tempted to reject it as mere resistance. Don't. Listen carefully and see if there is any validity to the points he is making.

If you determine that the person's statements about extenuating circumstance, or his arguments, are reasonable, then obviously you don't want to insist upon his compliance with your request. You would be making an exchange that's not in your self-interest, and you would be cutting yourself off from valuable information. Instead of pursuing the change, acknowledge the validity of the person's point, thank them for stating it, and either withdraw or modify your request.

When you tell Rick that you will let him leave early on Friday if all of the pending files are updated by noon on Friday, he flares up, reminding you that the deadline for the Ajax project he is working on is tomorrow. Rick warns that if he starts the file updating now, he'll miss the deadline. You check the schedule and see that he is indeed up against the wall.

Now that you know Rick's position, you might decide it is more important to have him complete the Ajax assignment than it is to have him start working on the files. Then you could politely withdraw your request by saying, "Thanks for reminding me about that, Rick. I definitely want you to follow the Ajax project through to completion. I'll figure out another way to get the files updated."

On the other hand, you might still want Rick to do the file updating, and you don't want to let him use Ajax as a way of completely avoiding the updating work. In this case, you could modify your request slightly: "Hmmm. I forgot about that deadline. Let's try this. I'll talk to Kim and get her to pull all the files, organize, and box them. That way, it will be easier for you to come in on Thursday and quickly do all the updating. Okay?"

If, after close examination, you determine that the other person's objections are just another version of the same resistance he's displayed during your last five attempts to get him to change, then it's time to move to Step 4.

CHAPTER EIGHT

How to Face Resistance—And Win

I f your request for change is met with pure resistance, you get what you want by gracefully going around the resistance. The techniques for side-stepping the resistor's tactics are easy to learn, easy to use, and best of all, they get results.

STEP FOUR: CIRCUMVENTING RESISTANCE TO CHANGE

There are several proven ways to circumvent the resistor's traps. Selecting which technique to use in a particular situation depends on the type of resistance you encounter. The most general all-purpose tool for bypassing resistance is called the Bamboo Technique, and it works like this.

The Bamboo Technique

When a typhoon rips through the tropics, rigid structures are torn away from their foundations and giant trees are uprooted, but the bamboo plant comes through unharmed. When hit with the force of the storm, it simply bends. Once the storm has blown itself out, the bamboo plant snaps back to its original position.

The resilient bamboo provides a great model of how to react when confronted with resistance. First, bend. Bend by acknowledging the other person's response to your request for change. Then, snap back. Snap back by restating your request. It's that simple. Bend. Snap back.

This two-step technique is dramatically effective because it lets the resistance blow by, leaving your change contingency in place and unaltered. Watch how the Bamboo Tactic counters name-calling and many other resistance tactics and helps create change calmly.

Name-calling. You've made your request for change and Esther has responded by saying that you're not taking her feelings on the matter into account. You don't defend yourself or extend the conversation. You bend.

"I can imagine, Esther, that it seems like I'm being insensitive. IF you will get this project done by the noon deadline, THEN I'll be happy to set aside an hour Friday to review your new campaign proposal."

"Perhaps I'm not always as sensitive as I should be. IF you finish the project by noon, THEN I'll be glad to . . ."

You can bend with virtually every harsh name people throw at you.

"In some situations I guess I can be an SOB. Here is what I am proposing. IF. . . , THEN . . ."

After a little practice, you'll be able to elaborate and increase the finesse with which you apply this technique.

"It's interesting that you say that about me. Lately, I too have been thinking that I've changed. I'll have to give that some more thought. Thank you for pointing that out. Now, IF . . . , THEN . . ."

Using "perhaps," "maybe," and "in some situations" enables you to acknowledge the resistor's response, without completely agreeing, but of course you can use whatever language suits your own style and the specific situation. Often, the change contingency sounds less blunt if you substitute the word "WHEN" for "IF." You can also state the THEN part of the contingency before mentioning the behavior you want in exchange. There are no set words, or necessary phrases, that you must use. Let the other person know that you heard what they said, and then quickly restate your change contingency. Avoid giving reasons, or elaborating, just stick to restating only your request.

Excuses. The bamboo tactic works just as well when you meet resistance in the form of excuses. Imagine the excuse for a delay is old equipment. Here's how you bend and snap back.

"I agree that using this old equipment can be time-consuming, and it would be easier if you had state-of-the-art equipment. When you complete this project, I'll be happy to . . ."

The annual report is due to be published at the same time you are asking for changes in a promotional campaign.

"I didn't realize your desk was that full, but if you put these changes through as I've asked, I'll be happy to delay my request for the new fliers until next Thursday."

The worker is too depressed by personal problems to work at top speed.

"I can imagine that it will be difficult to pull this off now. I'll be happy to let you leave two hours early that afternoon, if you will complete the audit by noon Friday."

The resistor must be able to see, as well as hear, your acknowledgment of their response. When you use the bamboo technique, you must not only listen, you must look as though you are listening. The acknowledgment should be a concise and accurate restatement of their response. It should be sincere. In some cases, you may even agree with the person. The purpose of the acknowledgment is to let the other person know that they have been heard, so that you can return to the contingency for change.

Emotional Displays. You've called individual meetings with the members of the lagging production department team. At your first meeting, Talia responded to your request for change with a clear show of anger. Here is the wind of resistance. This is your chance to bend like a bamboo reed.

"I can imagine that this isn't pleasant to hear, Talia. My goal isn't to upset you but simply to make a change that will improve things for both of us."

You've bent. You've acknowledged her response. Now you snap back with your request stated in the terms of the contingency for change.

"Now, when you . . . , then I'm prepared to . . ."

Try this out on Dabny, who responded to your request with a wounded expression.

"It looks as though this is disturbing to you, Dabny."

There's the bend. Here's the snapback.

"After you . . . , then I'll . . ."

For most of us, emotional outbursts—from tears to angry tantrums—are among the most difficult reactions to cope with effectively. The bamboo technique will help you feel more comfortable dealing with other people's emotions, and you'll be perceived as more warm and sympathetic, too.

If the person tells you his feelings ("This is very painful to me"), use his exact words in your acknowledgment. "It looks as though this is very painful for you." Alternatively, you can paraphrase the stated feeling. If he says this is painful, bamboo with, "I can imagine this is upsetting for you."

If the person communicates his emotions nonverbally, never explicitly saying what he is feeling, you can try to put words to those feelings. When someone cries, say, "I can imagine this is not pleasant to hear." If they communicate anger with a piercing stare, bamboo with, "This appears to be very disturbing to you. What I'm proposing is . . ."

When acknowledging an emotion, there is one phrase to avoid. Never say, "I know how you feel." We know what will happen next if you do.

They'll say, "No, you don't."

You'll say, "Yes, I do. I worked your job for the first six months after I started here."

They'll say, "It doesn't matter. You still don't know how I feel."

Irresistible force meets immovable object—ad infinitum. There goes any chance for producing change. Now you are talking about feelings, and your understanding of those feelings, instead of focusing on the change you want.

Never claim to know what a person feels. Stick with what you can see. "It looks as though this is . . ." Or use the phrase, "I can imagine . . ." Even with this wording, the person may tell you that you can't see or you can't imagine anything. What do you do? Go right back to the old bamboo.

"Perhaps I can't. Nevertheless what I'm suggesting is if . . . , then . . ."

When dealing with a resistor, you can express empathy by acknowledging the person's feeling, but still block protracted emotional displays by quickly restating your request for change. Recall that you have been patient and understanding of this person many times in the past. Now you want action.

Old Dogs. Harry says he can't incorporate these new techniques into his meetings because he has run his meetings as an autocrat for the last twenty years. The old way works for him, he says, and expecting him to change styles at this late date is ludicrous.

You can use the bamboo technique to get through to Harry.

"Harry, this new style may seem unnecessary, but if you will begin each of your next three staff meetings by encouraging people to voice any issues, problems, or ideas, then I will be happy to let you take those vacation days you requested."

Ingrid says she can't complete the employee evaluations because the numeric approach goes against her deepest values. People are too complex to be reduced to numbers, she protests. Besides, she is accustomed to the old way.

Again, you can empathize with her concern and still make your request.

"The new system is different and hard to get used

to, nevertheless I need your evaluations using the new system, by Friday at noon. When I receive them, I'll be happy to initiate the flex-time request you made.''

Criticizing the Method. You've stated your request and, in response, received a critique of your style. You can fuel the fire by defending yourself against the provocation, or you can simply bamboo and stay in control of the interaction.

"Did I sound extremely angry? Thanks for telling me. I appreciate your feedback. Let me just calmly repeat this proposal that will benefit both of us. If you will get those numbers up by the next reporting period, I'll be happy to reconsider your interim performance rating.''

"Did I say 'never'? Thanks for pointing that out. Never is too extreme a word; what I want to say is that when . . . , then . . .''

"I can see that my timing isn't quite right for you. But this is such a small thing I know we can handle it quickly now. If you will have this on my desk by noon tomorrow, then you can come in an hour later Thursday morning.''

Acknowledge that there may have been a problem with how, or when, you communicated your request. Acknowledge the other person's discomfort, indicate a willingness to change your tone, word use, or timing, and then snap back with your contingency for change.

Trivialization. Your request for change has been put into an expanded context so that it seems to be too unimportant to bother with. Once again, you can bamboo right past the resistance.

"Maybe, Joan, I am being shortsighted here. I'll give that some thought. In the meantime, if you will track down the record on that check from France we deposited with the bank, I'll see about getting you some temporary help with the 1099 forms."

"Kirk, perhaps I am splitting hairs on this. I'll give that some more consideration. Even so, if you will make certain that each delivery is inventoried at the receiving door, I'll be happy to put in your request for the new software."

Presumably you have actually given the person's charges some consideration in Step 3, when you evaluated whether they were reasonable or resistant.

You can increase your chances of getting agreement if you finish the contingency with a short question.

"If you finish all of the performance evaluations by noon on Monday, then I'll bend the rules and not report that you turned them in late. Okay?"

You can also end with "All right?" "Agreed," or "Do we have a deal?" Those little questions, when stated with optimism and confidence, smooth the way for the person to agree and simultaneously make it more difficult for the person to digress.

Wordfare. "That's a ridiculous idea. It doesn't make sense," Richard blurts out when you propose your change. Rather than falling into his trap and defending your proposal, or getting sidetracked by asking him to elaborate on the problems he sees, try bending.

"Richard, you're right. There are some potential problems with this approach, but what I'm saying is that if you'll research these invoices, and make certain the numbers are correct by next Wednesday, then I'll authorize the purchase of that monitor you need."

If Richard keeps arguing, bamboo again.

"If I gave you the impression there aren't some downside risks to this idea, then I apologize. Even so, if . . . , then . . .''

Too often we get caught acting as though our idea has no defects whatsoever. There is usually little harm in acknowledging that there are some potential counterarguments. Simply grant that there may be plausible reasons for disagreement, and then restate your request as part of the contingency for change.

Watch diplomats in negotiations, and watch the people in your organization who have reputations for handling conflict well. What do they do? In the face of disagreement, they graciously bend.

"The representative from Novaland has raised some very interesting points. And, you've given us a framework we can all use in our continuing discussions of the matter."

What has the diplomat really said? Nothing really. But by acknowledging contrary views he has avoided a fight. With a little practice, you too can gain a reputation as a good "people" person . . . the person to call when things get tense. In no time, you'll become the diplomatic leader in these situations.

Some polished performers will even pause to give consideration to a resistor's objection, before restating their request.

"Jessica, you raise an idea I hadn't thought of. Let me think about that for a second." Pause. "Very good point, that is a potential disadvantage to this approach. Even so, after consideration, I think the advantages outweigh the disadvantages, and I'm proposing that if . . . , then . . ."

When first learning to bamboo, many people inadvertently slip in an explanation with their snapback restatement of the contingency. Avoid explaining, because the resistor can easily pounce on your explanation and begin disagreeing with it. Keep it very simple. Acknowledge and restate.

Implementing the Bamboo Technique. With resolute resistors, you may have to bamboo more than once to get results. You've asked for a change and gotten fighting words in response. You bamboo.

"I can believe, Hume, that it seems like I'm moving too quickly on this, but if you will . . . , then I will . . ."

Hume responds, "Not only are you rushing this project, but you haven't given any thought at all to the extra time this is going to take."

You bamboo again.

"I realize we may be leaving you shorthanded on this, but if you will . . . , then I will . . ."

In most cases, simply bending and restating your change contingency once, twice, maybe even three times, will be enough to squelch the resistance. There is a limit to how many times you can bamboo, however, because you want to conclude the agreement in the allotted five minutes. If three bamboo responses to these kinds of resistance tactics doesn't yield results, it is time to move on to Step 5—the Resistance Contingency.

You'll find that in most cases the bamboo technique alone will yield quick results. Begin with a subordinate who keeps resisting. Plan ahead. Identify his typical resistance tactics, and rehearse your bamboo response on the ride to work. Then, when the occasion arises, bend with him.

If you've always reacted by fighting back, don't be surprised if mouths fall open when you openly acknowledge what the resistor says. Don't gloat. Bend, and then immediately restate your change contingency. Once you're comfortable acknowledging subordinates resistance tactics, move on to bambooing with peers and then, take on your superiors.

Postpone Extended Discussion

Raising extraneous issues to waste time and avoid change is another general strategy of resistors. They will, for instance, ask you to explain why you are making a request, link your request to larger more complicated topics, try changing the subject, or focus on the nature of your personal relationship rather than the content of your request. By alerting the person at the beginning of the discussion to the brief amount of time you have available, you set the stage for subsequently limiting the topics you will discuss. Like the Bamboo Technique, the Postpone Extended Discussion Technique begins with an acknowledgment of the topic the resistor is raising, but then asserts that the issue be discussed at a later time. It concludes with the same if-then change contingency. This technique is especially applicable to the following types of resistance.

Why? Why? Why? With a look of innocence and a tone of earnest inquiry, the resistor asks you to explain the logic behind your request. If you answer, he'll waste time by asking more questions. If you refuse to answer, or accuse him of attempting to distract you, he'll consume your time and energy by charging you of being defensive and incapable of explaining the reasons for your request.

If your knowledge of the person convinces you that his request is sincere, go ahead and briefly explain your thinking. But, if you think the person is trying to resist, then try this.

"I'm glad you asked, Sam, and I'll be glad to explain later. As I said, I have to get to the planning meeting at four o'clock, and that's just a few minutes away, so I can't explain fully. I'll be in my office tomorrow afternoon and will be glad to discuss the reasons then. Right now I want your agreement that you will rewrite the letter, and then I'd be happy to speak to Betty about your request for temporary clinical backup before the end of the month. Okay?"

Don't explain anything **now**. You want to postpone discussion on the subject until **later**. The resistor wants you to explain and convince him of the soundness of your request **before** he agrees to do it. His real goal is to keep you talking so that he can avoid doing what you want. Get the agreement before giving the explanation.

"Unfortunately I only have a minute and a half before that conference call, so I can't give you all the reasoning now. Check with my secretary and set up an appointment for later in the week. We can discuss more of the details then. At this time I want your agreement to . . ."

As always, greet the resistor's response—even though you judge it to be resistance—with a positive tone. You can even express pleasure at his inquiry.

Watch the seasoned politician when an interviewer hits him with a hard or embarrassing question. "I'm glad you've asked and given me an opportunity to set the record straight," he says. Of course the politician isn't the least bit happy, but he knows that it is in his self-interest to maintain that constructive upbeat demeanor.

Be prepared for the possibility of even more resistance when you attempt to postpone the discussion.

"So you expect me to do this even though I don't understand why?"

See. Another question. More resistance. He's trying to get you talking. Don't do it. Just use the Bamboo Technique and go right around it.

"I can imagine it's hard to do something when you still have some questions about it. Even so, because of the time constraints here, I would like you to agree to rewrite the letter now, and then we can meet later to go into my thinking on the matter. Agreed?"

With a little practice you can embellish the postpone technique. "Good question, Bill. That's the kind of analytic thinking we need in this group. I'll be pleased to explain my thinking, because I think teaching and explaining are an important part of my job. I think it's called mentoring these days, isn't it? Anyway. I'm on a real tight schedule right now, so we'll have to set up a time for later. Perhaps you could stop by around two or three on Friday afternoon? For now, I need your commitment to rewrite that letter this afternoon, and when you do, then . . ."

You should keep your word and meet with the person to discuss your reasoning, if he makes the effort to arrange the follow-up meeting. You already have him performing the changes you requested, but such a session will help you develop your own thinking, give the person greater ownership of the decision, and provide an opportunity to strengthen your relationship.

In fact, people seldom pursue these follow-up meetings. And when they do, an odd thing frequently occurs. A couple of hours before the appointed time, you may get a phone call "Look, some emergencies have come up, and I can't make it this afternoon at four. I still want to discuss that with you because I don't understand your thinking. It just can't be this afternoon."

It's amazing how frequently resistors cancel these meetings. Still, when you get this call, maintain the proper front with the resistor.

"Well, okay, Bill. Actually, your question got me to

do more thinking, and I've discovered even more reasons for making the change. Perhaps we can discuss all those at a time that would be more convenient for you. Give me a call."

Complicating Matters. Resistors will sometimes try to connect your request to a much larger issue in an attempt to get you bogged down in a topic of time-consuming, global proportions. The Postpone Technique works here, too. It begins with gracious acknowledgment of the subject the resistor is trying to introduce. Naturally you would be happy to discuss this too—later.

"Daryl, you raise a good point, and perhaps we should carefully examine the effect this will have on all of our manufacturing. To do justice to this issue, however, we'll need more time than I have right now. Let's plan a follow-up meeting to explore that. Right now, I need your agreement to . . ."

"That's an interesting idea. We don't take a broad historical perspective on many of our decisions. Given the time constraints we're operating under here, I'd like to get your commitment to make these changes now, and then we can examine the historical matters at our Friday meeting."

Don't argue or try to convince the resistor that his point is irrelevant. That simply wastes time by providing him with another issue on which he can expound. Acknowledge the possible relevance of his comment, and then assert that it be taken up later.

The valuable reward that you can offer in your change contingency enables you to set the order of topics on the agenda. If resistors want your resources, they'll agree to postpone the extended discussion.

Red Herrings. Another popular resistance tactic involves interjecting any of a thousand topics to confuse and exasperate you. With a little practice you can learn to avoid such tactics by postponing extended discussion until later.

"I hadn't thought about the effect this would have on the left-handed people, who are over six feet tall, and will be retiring within eighteen months. We may have time to discuss that over lunch tomorrow. Right now, what I need you to do is . . . , and when you do . . ."

"Perhaps this will be a problem that would be of concern to the shipping department as well, and we can explore it with them later. At this time, I'd like your agreement to . . . , then . . ."

"No, I didn't watch the game on TV last night, and I'd enjoy hearing your analysis of the mistakes the coach is making. If we can come to agreement on this immediately, there may be time to discuss the game. My proposal is that if . . . , then . . ."

As with the Bamboo Technique, you should reiterate your willingness to discuss issues later once, or twice, at most in any one encounter. If the resistor keeps insisting that his issue must be discussed before he agrees to act, then you switch to the bottom line countermeasure, the Resistance Contingency, which will be discussed in Chapter 9.

"I thought you were my friend." When resistors accuse you of not really being a friend, not caring about them, not acting like a brother, sister, father, spouse, etc., they are simply trying to distract you. Rather than agreeing to the changes you want, they try to change the subject to the nature of your relationship with them. A big time-consuming topic, indeed.

The Postpone Technique works well in these cases,

too, with one minor adjustment. The resistor is claiming that he knows your feelings better than you do. He doesn't, and you can gracefully tell him so.

"I do consider you my friend even though you don't think so. Our friendship is so important to me that I'm willing to meet with you anytime—after work today, early tomorrow morning—to discuss our friendship. Right now there is only time for us to agree on this small matter, and if you . . . , then . . ."

"You may feel that I don't appreciate all you have done for me, but I feel I do. I'd welcome an opportunity to discuss our different perceptions when we have sufficient time. Now, all we have time to do is agree that . . ."

Don't call him names or argue that he can't possibly know your feelings. That would simply be more grist for his time-wasting mill. Politely assert that your feelings are different than his. Even this may not be enough to stop him. He may retort:

"You don't know the first thing about friendship or gratitude."

He is making a last try to drag you off the subject. Since you have already made your point about your view of your feelings, you can now simply return to proposing a later time for more detailed discussion.

"It seems as though we have different concepts of friendship, and I'd really like to explore the similarities and differences in our views. Maybe we can do that after work today, or tomorrow. What I need now is your agreement to . . . then . . ."

In these cases, it is especially important to arrange a time to discuss the nature of your disagreement. If the person is a trusted friend, you should clarify any misunderstandings. Keep the topic of your friendship separate from the specific change you are requesting. By letting some time pass before the subsequent meeting, you give the resistor time to calm down. After a day or two, he may have come to accept the change you asked of him, and the extended discussion will be unnecessary.

Agree to Disagree

If Patrick, your chief of security, has a full head of steam up about conducting the sexual harassment training program with his people, bambooing may not be enough to quell his persistent resistance. When Patrick, or anyone else, keeps disagreeing with your request try one of these responses:

"It looks as though we're just going to have to agree to disagree on this one. You have your view and I have mine. That sometimes happens. Nevertheless, when you implement the training program with all of your staff, then I will . . ."

"This seems to be one of those situations in which reasonable adults come to different conclusions. It's not a question of whether I'm right and you're wrong, or vice versa. We just see things differently. What I'm proposing, is that if you will . . . , then . . ."

You don't have to be disagreeable to disagree. Calmly state that the two of you have different opinions without getting angry or denigrating the resistor's ideas. Anger will only throw you off track, which is the goal of the persistently arguing resistor. Cut the argument short by agreeing to disagree, and immediately returning to your change contingency.

Reinterpret Their Reaction

Some resistance responses send a hidden or double message. In such cases it's possible to circumvent the resistor's response by reinterpreting his message and giving it the best possible meaning. Catatonia provides a good illustration of how to use this technique.

Catatonia. You've made your request and your employee gives you a deadeyed, resentful stare. Instead of saying "yes," he says nothing. Usually we fall right into the resistors trap and interpret his lack of response as an emphatic nonverbal, "No Way."

We read meaning into his silence. We conclude that he hates our proposal and has no plans to do what we want. Before jumping to that conclusion, look and listen again. What has he actually said? Nothing. Why interpret this lack of response as disagreement? Why not reinterpret it as agreement?

"Marlon, I'm so glad you have no objections to my plan. I'll look forward to seeing your projections at the planning meeting next Monday."

"Good. I'm glad we don't have any disagreement about that. When you finish the report, I'll authorize that travel expense."

Using a positive tone of voice, simply reinterpret the lack of response as agreement and then restate the agreement or your contingency. Don't pause after your reinterpretation. If you do, you will give the person a golden opportunity to voice his disagreement. Don't give him that chance. Reinterpret positively and immediately initiate a new subject.

"Now the other thing I wanted to talk to you about is the upcoming retreat. I'd like you to play an active role in . . ."

"Next quarter there are some new marketing possibilities and I've been thinking you could make an important contribution. Here is what I was thinking . . ."

"I know you have some ideas about how we ought to handle the reorganization and I'd enjoy hearing your ideas now."

Have the next topic of conversation ready and move quickly and enthusiastically to it. The new topic should be something related to the self-interest of the resistor and should hold the promise of future benefits for him. This is similar to the technique salespeople use of assuming agreement on a deal. You simply assert that the person agrees and move on.

Your positive statement and enthusiasm will make it difficult for the resistor to voice disagreement, but you should be prepared for people who will now speak up. When you move on to the next subject, they'll protest:

"Whoa there. Slow down. I didn't say I agreed to do that. I think your idea is all wrong. First, . . ."

Don't despair. Notice what has happened. You have successfully broken their catatonia. They're talking and most likely they're voicing their disagreement with your request. But you already know how to deal with disagreement. Use the old Bamboo Technique:

"You raise some potential problems with my idea that we will have to bear in mind. Even so, if you will . . . , then . . ."

The times in your life when you must circumvent catatonia may be limited—unless you have teenagers, in which case it is a weekly calendar item—so you can plan your approach. When you do face a catatonic resistor, rehearse the language you will use in your reinterpretation of his silence. Prepare the next topic of conversation and be ready to bamboo in case he suddenly comes alive and disagrees with your reinterpretation.

Ambiguous Language. You can also use the reinterpret technique on resistors who give you ambiguous responses.

"I'm glad to hear you'll will try, and I assume that means the problem will be rectified by the end of work today. If it is, then I will be willing to change your vacation days."

"I know you are a man of your word, and that when you say you'll see what you can do, that means that you will make certain all those items are shipped by the end of each month. If they are . . . then . . ."

"Good. That's great. I'll look forward to seeing your completed report on my desk on Friday and giving you the afternoon off."

By expressing pleasure at their agreement, you are reinforcing your interpretation that they have agreed *to do* what you are requesting. Follow your expression of pleasure with a clear statement of the actions you now expect them to perform.

You can then remind them of the benefits of taking these actions by restating the change contingency. As with catatonia, it's useful to avoid any pauses which would provide an opportunity for them to disagree. Confidently move on to the next topic or simply end the meeting cordially and walk away.

Reluctant Acceptance. When you hit oil—quit drilling. That's the wisdom of wildcat oilmen, and it aptly applies to the double message of reluctant acceptance. Their words say yes, but their nonverbal communications say no, no, no.

In these cases, when you hear that "yes," don't

probe any deeper. Express pleasure that they have agreed, ignore their emotional messages of reluctance, and move on to the next subject.

It is natural when dealing with a good employee to be alert to subtle expressions of feeling and to try to clarify any problems. If a valued employee reluctantly agrees to complete an assignment, it makes sense to inquire about the source of her reluctance.

"Nancy, I sense that you are not wholeheartedly in agreement with my ideas. You have good business sense, so I'd really appreciate hearing your ideas before we implement this."

When reluctance is being used as a resistance tactic, the resistor is taking advantage of your disposition to be sensitive to expressions of emotion. The resistor can use your sensitive inquiry to sidetrack the discussion by raising a plethora of objections and a multitude of extraneous considerations. These are designed to waste time and distract.

Your judgment of whether the person's response is reasonable or resistant is crucial when it comes to reluctant acceptance. You are in the most informed position to decide if the person is sincere or simply playing a cat-and-mouse game with you—expressing reluctance so that you will invite them to vent their endless stream of counterarguments.

Defiant Acceptance. When resistors are rubbing their emotion in your face, you don't have to be a graduate of sensitivity training to see it. Their anger is readily apparent.

"Fine. That's just fine. If you want your stupid report, you'll get it."

"If you're ordering me to do it, and that's what I have to do to keep my job, then I'll do it."

These resistors want you to switch the focus of discussion onto their emotional displeasure. If you do, you will have played right into their hands.

We all know that the angry outburst is being used to communicate disagreement, but in fact the person has said "Yes." You hit oil. Quit drilling.

Act as though you don't even hear the anger. Publicly acknowledge the agreement and move on to the next agenda item. The error here is to respond to the emotional display. The most obvious mistake is to ask why the person is so upset. If you ask, he will tell you, and tell you, and tell you. Meanwhile your request will be lost in the dust.

Another disastrous counterresponse to this defiance is to chastise the resistor for getting angry. This, too, will lead to an unending discussion of his right to express his feelings, the defects of your idea, and the corresponding deficiencies of your leadership style. Worst of all, your comment gives him permission to engage in an emotional wrestling match.

Hard as it may be, act as though you are oblivious to the tantrum. Express pleasure, restate the change contingency and end the meeting. If you are a parent, you have no doubt used this approach with an unhappy child. It works with adults, too.

If you want to address the person's anger, do it at another time. Such expressions of defiance should not be tolerated as a routine part of normal work relationships, so put it on your list of behavior changes you will make in the near future, but not necessarily at this moment.

Using the reinterpret technique requires foresight and practice. As you note the kinds of tactics favored by the resistors in your world, pay particular attention to catatonia, ambiguous language, and reluctant or defiant acceptance. When you anticipate an encounter in which the person will use one of these devices, privately practice your response. That way you will be well drilled in exactly what to say. As usual, your manner should be civil and positive, and you should plan exactly what topic to move to next.

With a little planning and practice, you can do it. Keep your presentation constructive and just move right past the resistance. An added benefit is that, after using this approach a couple of times, resistors will realize that you won't react to their ambiguous messages, and they'll stop using them.

Get a Guarantee

There is no sweeter word than "yes," except when it is only pseudo-agreement. You make a request and the resistor promises to do exactly what you want, but, based on his past history, you suspect he won't follow through.

There is a way to get a solid guarantee of action when you hear these promises. The person is agreeing to take certain actions in the future, so you merely move your contingency into the future as well. It's done like this:

"Jimmy, I'm so glad to hear you say you will never talk to a customer in that manner again. That pleases me because this is really an important issue to me. I know you are a man of your word and you'll live up to this promise. But this matter is so important to me that I want to make certain that we completely understand each other on this. Let's say you slipped and did repeat this with another customer. I'm not saying you would,

I'm just saying hypothetically, what if you did. Let's both be clear that if you did then I would be forced to . . . [significant negative consequence]. Do we understand each other on that?"

Until now, your statements of the change contingency have always emphasized the rewards the person will receive if he does as you want. With pseudo-agreement, you need to bring out the negative half of the change contingency.

When you want someone to do something you dangle carrots. When you want them *not* to do something, you show the sticks. In this case, you speak hypothetically about something you don't want done, but you can still legitimately talk about potential negative consequences.

By repeatedly stating that you know the person will do as promised, you maintain a positive tone and eliminate any basis for him to say that you don't trust him. State that the extreme importance of the matter makes it necessary to spell out all the details. If he still tries to complicate matters by saying it is a matter of trust, you can blame your own obsession with the issue.

"I know you will live up to your promise. This is just so important to me that I want to make certain I dot all the i's and cross all the t's. Then, if the impossible does happen, we'll both know what the consequences will be."

Ultimately, there are no ironclad guarantees. You improve the chances of action, however, by getting the person to acknowledge what the negative consequence will be if he fails to keep his promise.

When you are in a strong power position with a subordinate, you can ask him what the negative consequences should be if he fails to fulfill his promise. This approach should be used sparingly. Reserve it for the rare cases in which you sense that the person is using resistance as part of a more general attack on your authority.

One advantage of letting the resistor set his own punishment is that he now owns part of the agreement. Frequently, he'll recommend a much greater consequence than you ever considered. If he tries to slip out by suggesting a minor or frivolous punishment, you can then restate the consequence you had in mind. Do it in all seriousness.

"Unfortunately, this isn't a joking or trivial matter. Obviously, I haven't made it clear just how important this is to me. Now, if you make this mistake again, then I'll be forced to . . ."

When you bring out the big guns here, you'll get quick agreement.

An Ounce of Prevention

Providing ground-level descriptions of the specific actions or outcomes you expect offers the best immunity against those who would try to put words in your mouth, or claim they don't understand the words from your mouth. By being specific, you block misunderstanding.

"Thank you for telling me of your confusion. What I'm saying is that I want you to take Tab A and insert it in Slot A, and when you do, then . . ."

You use the same technique when people attempt to recast your request "in other words."

"You're right, those are 'other' words. Let me make it as clear and concrete as I can. What I am saying is that if you will . . . , then . . ."

186

Begin by acknowledging that you may not have spoken with sufficient clarity, and then restate your change contingency with special emphasis on the specific behaviors you want the person to perform. Even when you suspect the person is only playing dumb, play it smart yourself and act as though you think they sincerely did misunderstand (once).

Too often we let the resistor's instrumental ignorance frustrate us to the point that we explode in disbelief and anger.

"How can you be so stupid? What am I paying you all this money for if you can't understand something as simple as this?"

Say that, and you've lost. The resistor provoked you into throwing the first punch and a gigantic name-calling argument is about to commence. Only later will you realize that you fell right into his trap, and he was able to avoid doing what you wanted.

Your goal is to get agreement to the change you requested within the five-minute deadline you announced earlier. While you are using these various circumvention techniques, the big clock keeps running. You can repeatedly use the techniques in a particular encounter so long as you don't go beyond that time limit. When you find yourself caught with an extremely persistent resistor, and your allotted time is about to expire, it's time for a stronger measure—the Resistance Contingency. This is the bottom-line technique for getting action.

CHAPTER NINE

The Bottom Line

With some people, no amount of bambooing, reinterpreting, agreeing to disagree, and postponing of discussion is going to stop their resistance. Each time you circumvent one of their tactics, they bounce right back with another one. If you don't apply the brakes quickly, they will continue to avoid change. In essence, you now have another behavior problem—endless resistance.

When your self-interest demands that a person quickly agree with your requested change, you must cut this resistance short. In these circumstances, you can use a variation of the if-then format, called the Resistance Contingency.

STEP FIVE: THE RESISTANCE CONTINGENCY

By using one resistance tactic after another, the individual is avoiding change and attempting to wear you down. Move on before he succeeds. You can block the resistor's attempt to drag out the discussion by introducing a new contingency.

"Rick, if we can't come to an agreement on this matter in the next thirty seconds, then I'll have no choice but to . . . (major negative consequence)."

State the IF half of the contingency with a tightly restricted time limit. Follow it with a precise statement of major negative consequences in the THEN half of the contingency—a clear declaration of the results of not reaching an agreement.

Using the Right Language

You can tailor the wording of the contingency to suit your own situation, but be certain to avoid condemning the other person. Don't say:

"Rick, all you are doing is bringing up one thing after another to avoid changing."

"I'm onto your game. You are just trying to waste time to wear me down. Well, I won't fall for it."

"All of these arguments you are raising are nothing more than resistance, and it's not going to work with me."

Accusing the person of resisting, or critically dismissing his responses may make you feel superior, but it will play right into his game plan. The resistor will now vigorously deny your accusations, express shock and hurt feelings, and even more heatedly counter your new allegations. Don't give him this new source of ammunition.

Focus the IF portion of your contingency on the necessity to reach an agreement, and be very precise about the time. Don't say we must resolve this "quickly" or "shortly." The persistent resistor will take advantage of any high-altitude ambiguity, so stay down at absolute ground zero.

Announcing the time as a specific number of seconds may at first seem harsh, and you may be tempted to propose a few minutes. But, if you say, "Look, I'd like to resolve this in the next two or three minutes . . . ," you know how long it will take . . . a minimum of three minutes. The hard-core resistor will push you to the limit of the time you give them, so keep it very short. Remember that you began by advising him that you only had five minutes for the whole encounter, so stick to that timetable.

Carrots and Sticks

The big difference between the regular contingency used in Step 2 and the resistance contingency lies in the "then" part of your request. While the change contingency always offers to reward the person if he does what you want, the resistance contingency threatens negative consequences if he does not stop a behavior.

As a general rule, rewards should be used to get someone to do something. The threat of punishment is reserved for those rare instances where rewards have not worked, and you must quickly stop an action that is having very detrimental consequences.

You want to get the person to stop wasting time with persistent resistance, so it is appropriate here to warn him of the negative consequences of continuing his unacceptable behavior. These consequences must be significant enough to outweigh the rewards he reaps by resisting your request, but they should not be excessively punitive. Your goal is an equitable exchange, not a hostile battle. If the other person, however, is going to inflict his costly resistance behavior on you, you may be forced to increase the costs he is incurring.

Maintain a Calm, Positive Manner

Your goal is not to be punitive, nor is it to demonstrate that you can be mean and tough. Your objective is to get his agreement. Adopting a macho manner with the few characters who will engage in this much resistance will only spur them to new heights of nasty counter-attack.

Therefore, when you state the resistance contingency, do so calmly and respectfully. There is no need to get emotional or to use harsh language. State the resistance contingency one time in simple language. "If we can't come to an understanding on this in the next thirty seconds, I'll be forced to . . . [negative consequence]."

Then transition back to your original change contingency.

"I don't want that and I don't think you do, either. That's why I'm suggesting that if you will . . . then I'll be glad to . . . What do you say?"

Or, "But that wouldn't be good for you and I wouldn't like it, either. Why don't we just agree to my proposal that if . . . , then . . . Okay?"

Using this polite and positive manner may seem strange at first. Most of us think that we have to adopt a fierce and threatening demeanor when we warn someone of the dire consequences of their continued misbehavior. We mistakenly think that if we look tough enough, we'll be able to intimidate the person into stopping their evil deeds. Usually our ferocity just prompts them to greater pugnacity, and the encounter escalates into an antagonistic shouting match, which ends in a fight and lingering hard feelings.

When you warn the resistor of the negative consequences of not reaching rapid agreement, don't worry about having to talk loud enough so that he'll hear it. Negative consequences grab people's attention. He will hear it, and sometimes that is all that is needed. Some resistors are just testing you to see whether you are sufficiently in control to use negative consequences. The moment you unsheathe the sword, they will quickly agree with your request.

People who truly are in positions of power don't have to rant and rave. Since they control resources that really matter to the other person, they can warn of the impending negative consequences in a calm manner. Instead of adopting an imposing demeanor to awe the resistor, let the content of your contingency do the work.

Just discuss the matter civilly and sensibly. Concisely state the resistance contingency with a smile on your face and confidence in your voice, and then ask for his agreement on the change contingency that you initially proposed.

Remember you are in a high power position here. You have waited for a time when the other person really wants something from you, so if he is unwilling to agree you can walk away from the encounter at any time. And, if you were to calmly walk away, he would lose more than you would.

Planning for the Resistance Contingency

Knowing in advance exactly what negative consequences you will use in the resistance contingency is critical. If you wait until the situation arises to construct the resistance contingency, you will either not be able to think of a suitable negative consequence, or you will impulsively threaten some extreme measure ("if you don't shut up, you're fired") you are not prepared to follow through with.

Plan ahead so you are prepared for this worst-case scenario. When you are identifying your resources in the planning stage, you should specify for yourself both the positive consequences you are going to use in the change contingency and the negative consequences you are going to use in the resistance contingency. Draw from the resources over which you have decision-making control. Knowing you are prepared with the exact statement you'll use if the person does persist in resisting your request will also give you the confidence to carry off the whole encounter with calm certainty.

The negative consequences can take one of two forms. They can be negative either because they are inherently aversive to the person, or they can be negative because the person loses a positive benefit that he had been receiving.

The first category includes taking an action that would clearly be undesirable for the other person. This may mean making a negative entry in his performance evaluation file, restricting or prohibiting him from participating in upcoming projects, ruling him out as a candidate for promotion or added responsibilities, or, in extreme cases, temporarily suspending him from work.

The second source of negative consequences is all the positive things you are already doing for the person. If he continues to resist, you could withdraw many of the rewards you have been providing him. Since you are probably already doing a great deal for this person, you have a large inventory of resources to work with here. The long list of small favors, educational assistance, perks, and rewards you confer on the person are potential sanctions. Having a clear idea of exactly what good things you have been doing for the other person will give you specific ideas about the things you might potentially take away.

Adopt the same constructive tone whether you are warning about imposing a punishment or rescinding a benefit.

"If we can't resolve this matter in the next thirty seconds, then I'm not certain that I'll be able to continue to include you in my executive council group. Obviously, I value the contribution you make in those meetings, and that's why I hope we can come to a satisfactory agreement on my original proposal that if . . . , then . . ."

After restating your original request, be quiet and be prepared. Most people will quickly agree upon hearing the negative consequences of continued resistance. When they do, you can smile, express pleasure at their agreement, and move on to Step 6.

What If They Are Still Resisting?

There will be a rare few who will use your Resistance Contingency as the basis for even more resistance.

"Oh, thirty seconds, huh. That's your problem. Everything has to be decided on the spur of the moment."

"Nice, very nice. You won't even tolerate any discussion. It's always your way or else."

Here comes more resistance, and you know how to deal with it. Simply return to the circumvention techniques you used earlier.

"Thirty seconds isn't very much time, but I think it is sufficient for us to come to agreement on my proposal that if you . . . , then . . ."

"It's true that I don't have time now for extended discussion on this point. I'd be happy to spend more time on it with you later. Right now I would like your agreement that if . . . , then . . ."

When you use negative consequences in a contingency, you open yourself up for a particular type of resistance that can be very destabilizing at first.

"Hey, I don't like threats or people who make them."

"Don't point a gun at my head."

"Don't try backing me into a corner."

Being accused of making a threat, pointing a gun, or cornering people can be unnerving because we don't usually like to have people characterize us as harsh and uncompromising. But of course, these dramatic overgeneralizations are just another form of resistance. You can handle them with a slight variation of a response you already know—the bamboo technique. Partially acknowledge what the person is saying, and then refocus the discussion on the rewards he will receive from agreeing to your original request.

"I can imagine that it may seem like a threat, but my basic proposal is a positive one that can benefit both of us. If you would be willing to . . . , then I'd be happy to . . ."

When you use the resistance contingency, you must be prepared to deflect the barbs and other diver-

SIX SIMPLE STEPS FOR GETTING RESULTS

sions the person may try to throw at you. This time, though, strictly limit how long you will bamboo.

Enforcing the Resistance Contingency

When the thirty seconds expire, you must enforce your resistance contingency. This can be done in the same calm positive manner that you have been using up to this point. As the old saying advises, you don't have to be disagreeable to disagree.

"Rick, I'm very sorry that we couldn't come to an agreement on this matter. This means I won't be recommending you for . . ."

Express your regret at his failure to agree, indicate you will be enforcing the resistance contingency, say goodbye, and immediately engage in the next task. If you said you had a call to make, begin dialing. If you said you had a meeting to attend, gather your materials and head off down the hall. These actions coupled with your calm, confident statement, will reinforce the resolution behind your decision.

Very few encounters will proceed to this point. In the rare one or two cases that do, you may think you've completely lost your chance to get the person's agreement. You haven't.

Individuals who will go this far are usually testing to see if you will actually stand behind your contingencies. If you clearly indicate that they have lost the opportunity to get the original benefit and are now going to incur a cost, they will almost invariably give in.

"Perhaps I was too hasty in rejecting your proposal. . . ."

"Look, I'm sorry I let my emotions get the best of me. Can't we still work out an agreement? I'm willing to . . ."

"Please don't get angry or do anything rash. I don't like it, but I'm willing to go along with what you are asking. This isn't so important that I want to risk my whole future with the company."

Don't be surprised if you see the resistor figuratively drop to his knees. When he does, avoid the two major mistakes people often make. First, you may feel so sorry for the person that you reduce, or withdraw, your change request as a means of sparing him pain.

"Okay, look, it isn't that big a deal. I didn't know it would upset you so much. We'll keep things as they are for now, but next week I expect you to . . ."

Don't fall for this last show of emotions. You wouldn't have asked for this change if it wasn't necessary, and if you back away from it now, you'll only have to try for it again in the future. Think back to your original goal in this situation. You wanted to produce the change, not demonstrate what a compassionate person you are.

The second error people make when they clearly have the advantage over the person is to make even more demands. You might be tempted to up the ante while you're in the high power position. Don't. The goal is equity in your relationships, and your initial offer involved a trade of equally valued actions. Stick to your initial equitable offer.

The person may not immediately adopt a position of supplication at your feet, but as you walk him to the door, he'll reconsider his recalcitrance. In extreme cases, he'll keep up the tough resistant front until he goes back to his office, and then you'll get a telephone call in which he gives his reluctant agreement. In one instance, an employee's spouse called a manager at home in the evening and said, "Bill has been thinking about what you said, and he has decided to go along with your request.''

If all else fails, you must follow through with the action you warned of in your resistance contingency—and the sooner, the better. Otherwise, you'll be known as a paper tiger and this guy, and a lot of others, will begin resisting any and all of your requests. As long as you have planned well, and correctly selected rewards and costs that are of real value to the other person, virtually no encounter will run this full course. But you must be prepared to act if the worst case becomes reality.

STEP 6: CLOSURE

When the person does agree to make the changes you are requesting, your next move is to get closure on the whole deal. This final step is designed to increase the likelihood the individual will do exactly what he has said that he would.

Restate the Agreement

In cases in which the person has resorted to several resistance tactics before agreeing, it's a good idea to express pleasure at his agreement, and then restate the agreement.

"Rick, I'm glad to hear that you agree with my proposal. Let's both be clear on exactly what we have agreed to. You will complete updating all the files by noon Friday, and if you do then I'll let you take Friday afternoon off. Okay?''

Simply restate the details of the change contingency and ask for his agreement. In situations where you think the person won't live up to the verbal agreement, it may help to put the agreement in writing, and then both of you can sign it. Another alternative is to let the resistor state the agreement in his own words first. Correct him if he stated anything incorrectly, and then indicate your concurrence.

In the restating of the agreement, you may be tempted to go for a little more. Since the person has already agreed, you know you are in a strong position, and you may find yourself adding in a few more embellishments. Don't. Keep it straightforward and equitable by simply restating your original proposal.

Getting Verbal Acceptance

When you restate the agreement, close with a question.

"Okay?"

"Agreed?"

"Is that right?"

Nod your head up and down slightly in agreement as you ask this closing question and then watch and listen carefully.

Most people will agree immediately. When they do, express pleasure at their agreement, no matter how many times you had to bamboo. Keep the tone positive.

There is an interesting minority, however, whose response to your question will be to mumble something that may sound like yes but is completely garbled. Others will give you an ambiguous nonverbal acknowledgment. Their heads will bob around in several directions at once. Still others will only raise an eyebrow or give you an exaggerated smile.

Why do people resort to all these ambiguous signals instead of coming right out and saying, "Yes. Agreed"? They do it because even here, at the very end, they are trying to find an escape route. People are amazing. If you settle for the indecipherable vocalization, or the nonverbal acknowledgment, you will probably be disappointed later.

Imagine that Rick has only ambiguously signaled his consent to complete an assignment in one week. When the files aren't completed by Friday at noon, you go to Rick to inquire about what happened.

"Rick, you said you'd complete the project by noon?"

We all know what Rick will say: "Oh no, no, no. I didn't *say* that I would have it finished."

To avoid experiences such as these, explicitly ask for unambiguous verbal agreement. If the person resorts to ambiguous language, or a noncommittal nonverbal response, say something such as:

"I'm not certain exactly what you are saying. Are you saying yes?"

"You're nodding your head. Are you saying yes?"

By exaggerating the statement of the yes, and nodding your head up and down, you guide the person to verbally commit himself. Repeat these questions once or twice until the individual explicitly agrees. Then you can smile and state your pleasure at the agreement.

Some people like to seal an agreement with a handshake. This is effective because the clear public handshake can be referred to in the future if one party fails to live up to his end of the bargain: "Rick, if you'll recall, we both agreed to this and shook hands on it."

Almost everyone will publicly express their agreement to the contingency, even if they have to be nudged a bit. If, at the last minute, the individual tries to slip out of the agreement, you should calmly express regret that he is unwilling to agree, and withdraw your offer. Your obvious resolve not to give him the reward he desires will produce the words you want to hear.

Getting the individual to verbally agree to your contingency doesn't guarantee that he'll live up to his word, but it helps. You have closed one more loophole that he could have used to avoid changing.

Build for the Future

The positive mood associated with your agreement creates an ideal opportunity for you to shape how you want people to communicate with you in the future.

"Rick, I'm glad we reached an agreement, and I'm glad we were able to do so quickly. Our discussion focused on the specifics, we didn't get caught up in tangential issues, and we were able to agree very quickly. That's what I consider to be good communication.

"It's the kind of thing that makes me want to work with someone. In the future when I think about who to bring in on new projects, your name will come to mind because I know we can communicate so efficiently.

"You seem to understand that there are times when I can't afford to talk at length, and that I need your quick agreement. That's not my usual style, but sometimes it's necessary. I appreciate your cooperation and look forward to working with you in the future. Thanks."

By praising his communication practices—being specific, not digressing, agreeing quickly—you are reinforcing what the individual has done and letting him know how you want him to deal with you in the future. By honestly saying that his behavior makes you want to work with him in the future, you let him know he can reap future benefits if he maintains the same habits of communication.

A statement such as this is obviously only appropriate when the person has agreed quickly. If you've had to bamboo repeatedly, or were driven to use the resistance contingency, you can take this opportunity to shape future communications, but you word it differently.

"Rick, I'm glad we reached agreement. Our discussion here suggests an idea that I'd like to try in the future. I prefer discussions where we stay focused on specifics, that concentrate on one subject, and where we arrive at agreements quickly and harmoniously. That's what I call good communication.

"I prefer to talk things out, but occasionally I can't afford extended debate or discussion. In those situations, what I need is quick agreement. I like to work with people who understand that sometimes we simply must reach an agreement quickly.

"It is people who communicate in those ways that I enjoy working with. When I think about who to bring in on new projects, I think of people with whom I can communicate efficiently. With your ability and experience, there are many areas where you could make important contributions, helping the company and yourself in the process. I want to prominently include you in those kinds of projects and if, in the future, we can communicate in the efficient and effective way I've just described, then your name will definitely come to mind when I'm thinking about future assignments. Thanks again for your agreement here."

You should emphasize the specific communication

practices in which you want him to engage in the future, coupled with the reminder that you expect quick agreement in these situations. Avoid criticizing specific forms of the resistance the individual engaged in during the prior discussion. Focus on the future and mention his positive attributes. Maintain the same respectful, calm, and positive manner, but be ready to bamboo if he tries to make an argument out of these closing remarks.

"So, are you saying I didn't stick to the point, and that I'm just supposed to keep my mouth shut, and not say what I think? That's not the kind of person I am."

"No, no Rick. I'm sorry I gave you that impression. I'm talking about the future, not the past, and making constructive suggestions that would benefit both of us. I value you as a thoughtful person who likes to give issues full consideration, but there are times when decisions and agreements must be reached quickly. At those times, I appreciate people who understand the demands of the moment, and are willing to go along with my suggestions. We can always talk at length later. As I said, I'm bringing this up because I do value your talents, and think there are many ways we can work effectively together that will help both of us."

Almost every discussion of effective interpersonal relations stresses the importance of good communications, and rightly so. Here at the conclusion of your change request, you have an ideal opportunity to concretely improve the way people communicate with you. You don't have to mimic language in the above examples verbatim. Use words that suit you. Regardless of how you say it, let the person know the specific ways you want him to communicate, and let him know that he will be rewarded for his efforts.

In taking these final moments to make specific recommendations about how you want him to communicate, you are also reducing future resistance. By urging him not to engage in the resistance tactics he just used, you are showing the individual how to reap more benefits and more rewards out of his relationship with you. It will also make the working relationships more rewarding to you.

Living Up to Your Promises

Be certain to follow through with the rewards you promised in your change contingency. When the other person performs the actions you requested, you should gladly give him the resource you offered in exchange.

Just as you must never make a threat that you won't enforce, so you should not make a promise that you will not fulfill. You are, in effect, making a promise in your change contingency because you are saying that if the person does what you want, then you will do what he wants. Too often, people make this promise and then don't live up to it.

Most of us know that unhonored promises ruin your credibility and no one will deal with you in the future. People sometimes try to avoid or postpone the cost of giving the other person the promised rewards by pointing to a crisis or exceptional circumstance. They use their smooth talk and tales of woe to justify why they can't deliver. They attempt to avoid present costs by promising even greater rewards in the future.

"Look, Rick, I know that I said you could take Friday off if you completed that report, but I just got a call from our Minneapolis client, and they are threatening to terminate our contract if we don't get that work out to them. I can't afford to give you a whole day off in the middle of this crisis. Just work with me on this one, and I'll give you two days off when we get through it.''

Perhaps this is an exceptional crisis, but it's more likely that when the Minneapolis crisis ends, there will be one in Texas. Or, there will be an extreme expense that has destroyed the budget, so there isn't any money for the promised raise or bonus.

When we are in a position of power it is easy to fall into the trap of breaking our initial promise. We have the change we want and now giving something in return doesn't seem so important anymore.

You may get away with this once or twice at the office, but people will soon learn that you are not to be trusted. The resulting loss of credibility will mean that your future change contingencies won't work, no matter how well you follow the advice in this book—and you won't get the results you want. You must live up to your promises and give people the rewards that you said you would.

If you don't give the promised rewards, you are the one who is making the relationship inequitable. The change you requested required the other person to incur a cost and give you a reward. At that moment in time, the relationship is inequitable to his disadvantage. If it stays that way, not only is he going to be unhappy, he is going to do something about it. If you don't deliver, he is going to start inflicting costs on you. It's in your self-interest to keep all relationships equitable and profitable for everyone concerned.

POSTSCRIPT: HANDLING THE MOST SERIOUS CASES

The tools in this book are designed to handle those periodic instances of resistance we all encounter from people who are generally good performers but who are resisting a particular change request. These same tools can do more. You can use them to solve those extreme cases of dismal, or deteriorating, work performance that seem resistant to every management technique invented. You can use them to turn around the performance of those few people whose performance is clearly below par.

When you are ready to begin the change process with someone who needs to make a great many changes, plan a meeting to lay the groundwork for these major changes. Here are some suggestions on how to conduct such a meeting:

You've just been named production chief. Along with a number of benefits, high expectations, and an expanded workload, you've inherited a line foreman, Archie, who is every manager's worst nightmare.

His line group consistently produces less than the other groups, has a higher reject rate, and a higher absentee rate. Archie has a reputation for sabotaging managers who try to interfere with his methods, a nasty temper that flares whenever extra production demands are made, and a crew that's loyal but looks like a bunch of scared rabbits. Furthermore, Archie has a brother who is a labor law specialist, and he's not shy about letting you know it. Archie has staked out his own inviolable turf, and God help you or anyone else who presumes to trespass on it.

Initiate the process of change with Archie in a private meeting in which you frame all the changes you are going to be making. Although you can assume that your intervention will have a positive outcome, it is always wise to integrate the company's personnel officer into any circumstance where disciplinary action, or dismissal, may be the final result. This will ensure that the company's legal position and the employee's rights are respected as you put your plans into action.

You have three primary goals to accomplish in this initial meeting. First, you must advise Archie that his current performance is not acceptable, but that you firmly believe he is capable of making it so. Second, you must demonstrate to Archie that you are committed to helping him achieve that goal. Finally, you must set the framework in which all your interactions with Archie in the near future will take place.

"Archie, I have been impressed with many of the things you've done here, and I want to work with you to achieve even more. I want to talk with you about your overall performance and the ways it can be improved.

"We'll go into the details of that in a minute, but I want to let you know that I am committed to helping you get your overall job performance up to where it needs to be.

"We're going to work on the deficient areas beginning now so that we can avert the possibility of serious negative repercussions for you if your performance does not improve. If we work together, we won't have to worry about them at all."

Don't make explicit threats at this point, or specify the possible negative consequences to which you have alluded. Even if Archie asks exactly what they are, avoid discussing them. Concentrate on the areas that need improvement and on the importance of improving.

"Archie, I see several areas where change is going to be essential. Productivity on your line needs to come up to the average set by the other lines. The reject rate has to be below 1 percent. And work attendance must improve to meet the 5 percent absentee threshold the company has established."

As you specify the areas that most need improvement, Archie will undoubtedly begin to offer excuses and arguments, feign ignorance, or display any of a variety of other resistance tactics. Bamboo each time, returning to your specification of needed changes.

When you've outlined the areas that need improvement, describe what you're willing to do to help. You'll help Archie specify each incremental change that needs to be made. You'll help him define specific goals and timelines for their accomplishment. You'll teach him the skills he lacks, or assign someone appropriately qualified to do so.

Specifying the areas of improvement sets the general guidelines for the **"if"** portion of the change contingencies you'll be initiating after this preliminary meeting. The things you're willing to do to help can potentially serve as some of the rewards for the **"then"** portion of subsequent contingencies.

Keep your tone serious but positive. Repeat your statement of commitment to these changes and reiterate your confidence in successful results. Before pursuing the specifics of the changes, ask Archie for his commitment. "Are you willing to work with me on this?"

If he hesitates or says no, suggest that he give your

proposal some thought. "I realize this is a lot to digest. Why don't you think about all we've discussed, and we can meet at 7:30 tomorrow morning and see where we go from there."

After having some time to mull over the possible negative consequences of continued resistance and the positive consequences of changing, he may be willing to commit to your proposal. When you meet in the morning, ask immediately for his decision.

If this second meeting with Archie finds him still unwilling to commit, you'll have to resort to the resistance contingency. Spell out the serious negative consequences he will suffer if he does not begin to change within the specified time. Then restate your willingness to work with him to make the necessary improvements.

Archie may counter your resistance contingency with arguments and threats. No doubt he'll mention his brother, the attorney, in a menacing manner. Bamboo and return to your proposal for change.

"Archie, I can appreciate that you may find these possibilities unpleasant. I want to emphasize that they don't have to happen. If you'll commit to a plan to bring your performance in line with what I've outlined, I'm willing to help you get there. What do you say?"

If you still haven't persuaded Archie to commit to changing, end the meeting quickly, but politely. With guidance from your company personnel office, initiate the actions necessary to document Archie's failures to perform.

You must now follow through on the serious negative consequences that you mentioned to him. As you document and notify Archie of his performance deficiencies, it will become abundantly clear that you were serious. At this point, Archie may decide to accept your earlier offer.

If he does, congratulate him and get on with the business of making changes. Once you've gotten Archie's commitment, you move into the role of coach. You guide and advise, but he does the bulk of the work. Help Archie list the necessary changes and set appropriate time frames and quantifiable standards for measuring progress.

The time limits you establish for his performance to come up to acceptable levels should be reasonable but as short as possible. You don't want Archie using gradualism as a resistance technique in itself. Be prepared to squelch his occasional backsliding as he tests your resolve. Once Archie starts to make progress, and he sees your commitment in action, his turnaround will accelerate.

Your Action Plan

CHAPTER TEN

Making Change Happen

This chapter provides a series of exercises to help you break loose from bad habits and incorporate the change-producing tools and techniques described in this book into your daily interactions. You'll need five file folders—one for each of five key people in your business life—paper, and pencil. As you work through this chapter, you'll be adding pages to the folders that will help you refine your skills and pave the way for the changes you want. The value of the exercises results from doing them, not from thinking about them, so please practice the recommended actions. You won't be disappointed.

ANALYZING PEOPLE'S ACTIONS

An easy way to begin sharpening your analytic skills is to observe other people's behavior and explanations. Take out your pencil and paper and, for each of your five people, write descriptions of how they usually act. It's okay to use general labels at first. Think about how they act and talk when they are "in character." Once you have these baseline descriptions, switch your focus to the times when they act "out of character."

The point of this exercise is to become aware that people have both the knowledge and the capacity to behave in markedly different ways. As you become increasingly familiar with the fact that people's behavior does change, you'll become more convinced that you too can prompt them to change.

There are two judgments we tend to make about people acting inconsistently, that can cloud our clear observation. First, when we see someone acting differently than they normally do, we often discount the observation. "That's not really him," we say. Or, "He just acts that way when the head honchos are around." This judgment causes us to overlook the fundamental fact that the person is capable of radically and quickly changing his behavior.

Second, we sometimes condemn people who act very differently from one situation to the next. We call them fickle, or unreliable, but we fail to consider the implication that they have the capacity to quickly alter their actions. For now, suspend your judgment and focus on observing how much people can, and do, change the way they behave from one time to another.

The Causes of Behavior

As you write down your observations of how differently your five key people behave in different situations, look for the characteristics of the situation that might have prompted their behaviors. You may find one person is warm and gregarious with customers, but distant and reserved with subordinates. Another person might play dumb with her superiors, yet demonstrate a quick and keen grasp of topics brought to her by the people she supervises. Analyze how each different response pays for the person in the particular situation.

Pay special attention to the reasons people give for their own behavior. Notice how frequently they attribute their actions to psychological factors.

You hear a co-worker complaining that the boss never lets anyone participate in decision making in your unit. This irritates him, he says, because he really *wants* to participate, he would *feel* more like an adult if he were allowed to participate, and he *needs* to sense that he has some sort of control over his own professional life.

He has cited a number of psychological causes of his desire to see a change in the decision-making process. Look beneath the surface of this kind of rhetoric and try to identify the consequences that would result from the change he is advocating. If he had more of a say in decision making, he might be able to get his assignment altered, his responsibilities expanded or contracted to his benefit. Or, he might be able to position himself for advancement. Go beyond the purely psychological to identify the more tangible benefits your colleague may be seeking.

On another piece of paper, list the explanations each of your five people commonly give for their own actions in one column. Note how frequently they explain their actions by invoking beliefs and values ("I think this is the only fair thing to do"), their personality or character ("I always try to give people the benefit of the doubt") or their feelings ("I've just got a gut reaction on this one").

In an adjacent column, list what you see as the tangible consequences of their actions, or the position they advocate. Most of the time, you can immediately see that the position they held, or the action they took, yielded positive consequences for them. At other times you'll have to push your thinking, and it may take a while, to discover their hidden payoffs. Be patient. When you hear these psychological explanations, try to identify how the behavior actually benefits the person. Identify what the real-world consequences of the action will be, and see if those consequences serve the individual's self-interest.

GETTING DOWN TO GROUND LEVEL

The most important skill you can develop to produce change is the ability to precisely state the actions, or outcomes, you desire from other people. Talking specifically, at ground level, will help other people know exactly what you want, and will block potential resistors from claiming that they didn't understand your request.

Take out paper and pencil, and define one of the people problems you face in your own work situation. Write the problem in your own words to begin with and then restate it in more and more concrete terms. Try to define exactly what you want the person to stop doing. Keep asking, *"What do I want this person to stop doing?"*

After you have identified what you want him to stop doing, write down what you want him to do. Ask yourself, *"What do I want him to do?"* Write down the answers. Read your answer and hunt for ambiguous words that need to be further specified.

If you get stuck at the higher altitudes in clouds of generalities, change your approach slightly. Try to identify when the problem behaviors are most costly to you. Ask, *"In what situations are his actions most problematic?"* By thinking about different real-life situations, you can often picture exactly what the person is doing, or not doing.

If those questions don't get you down to specifics, try asking yourself what your best employee would do in one of these situations. If you can describe the actions of the ideal employee in ground-level language, then you can use those same descriptions to specify what you want your problem person to do. Incidentally, don't make any reference to this ideal employee when you ask for the change. Such a public comparison pulls the conversation away from your request and invites resistance.

Another way to practice ground-level communication is to use other people's descriptions of their people problems. As you listen to someone tell you about their latest problem case, mentally restate his complaints in terms of specific actions. You can help the other person clarify his problems by asking him the same kind of behavioral questions you're asking yourself.

"I think I understand what you mean, but could

you give me a specific example of what he does that you dislike?"

"If you were to specify one particular thing you want him to do differently, what would it be?"

"How would he act if he was more like you want him to be?"

Your questions will help the other person more clearly understand what he wants, and you can hone your own analytic and interpersonal abilities. The learning curve for this skill rises very quickly. Soon the transition from high-altitude synonyms and psychological jargon to ground-level behavioral language will become an automatic part of your problem-solving.

ANALYZING YOUR RELATIONSHIPS

How good, or bad, are the five key relationships in your business life, and what should you do about each? On another piece of paper, draw two crossing lines to divide the page into four equal boxes. Label the upper left box "My Rewards," and the one below it "My Costs." Use the other person's name and label the upper right box "X's Rewards" and the lower right one as "X's Costs."

Take five or ten minutes during the next two weeks to fill in the specific rewards and costs that are exchanged in each relationship. If you find you have described rewards in high-altitude language, use the questioning technique to bring them down to specifics.

These analyses will enable you to determine whether each relationship is equitable or inequitable, where inequities lie, and how the relationship can be rebalanced. If it's equitable, you should give yourself a pat on the back and seek to preserve that equity. You might also take a moment to tell the other person how much you value the relationship.

You may find that a relationship is inequitable in your favor. Your ratio of rewards to costs is greater than the other person's. If this is the case, the other person is probably unhappy. You should start immediately doing things to restore equity in the exchange. You might go to the person, express your pleasure at all he has done for you, and ask if there is any way you could show your gratitude in a concrete way. If he makes some reasonable requests, thank him for telling you and graciously give him what he wants. If he asks you for things that seem excessively costly to you, and that might tilt the inequity in his favor, propose a compromise that will, in your analysis, restore equity.

When the inequity is to the other person's advantage and to your disadvantage, don't just get upset. Get specific about what you want to do to restore equity. Go to your page with the four boxes, and list the rewards you want the other person to start giving you. Drop down to your cost box, list the costs he is inflicting on you (for example, always complaining, making sarcastic remarks), and specify the things you want him to stop doing.

You now have two lists you can use in preparation for trades with the inequitable partner. You have identified the rewards you want, and the things you will ask him to stop doing because they are costly to you. These are the behaviors you will include in the IF part of your requests, the next exercise will enable you to fill in the THEN portion of your contingencies.

IDENTIFYING YOUR RESOURCES

You have already identified a number of your resources when you filled in the box of rewards you are
currently giving the other person. An easy way to expand your list of the many resources you possess is to
simply start keeping track of the things people ask you
to do. Add another piece of paper to the files you've
started for each of the key people in your life. For two
weeks, write down every single thing they ask you to
do.

By the end of two weeks, you will discover that
people want a great many things from you. You possess huge resources, so you're in a great position to
start trading for the changes you want. You may also
find that you've been giving things away free without
even realizing it. Now that you can see all the valuable
resources you have been giving away, you can be more
careful to get a fair trade in return.

Watch closely for patterns and you'll see that some
people consistently ask you for the same kinds of
things. A subordinate regularly asks you to bend the
rules, a peer is repeatedly requesting assistance with
his written reports, and your boss unfailingly asks you
to handle irate clients. Being able to predict what kind
of resources particular people repeatedly ask for will
enable you to plan ahead and form your contingencies
in advance. You can anticipate when and what they
will want from you and insert those resources in the
THEN part of the contingencies you will use in making
trades.

Your list for some people might remain blank.
Some of the key people in your life may never ask you

for anything. This means you are in a low power position with them, and your capacity to get them to change is limited. There is still hope.

These key people who don't seem to want anything from you may be able to uncover your resources for you. Businesses pay people to find out what their customers want so that they can better serve them and earn a profit in the process. You can do it, too. Just ask.

"What can I do to make your job easier?"

"Is there anything in that project I could help you with?

"How can I make this a more pleasant place for you to work?"

This can be done casually or in a formal planning and goal-setting session. Meeting individually with subordinates, peers, and even superiors to find out their needs will enable you to help them and to help yourself.

Begin sharpening this skill by questioning people with whom you already have an equitable relationship. Tell them you're just exploring options—you don't need to start proposing changes immediately. This will give you a chance to practice, and it will build your confidence before you approach the people with whom your relationship is inequitable.

Handling Difficult Requests

As you talk with more people, you may begin to worry that this was a bad idea. You just know someone is going to take this opportunity to ask you for the moon. In fact, very few will. Most people are reasonable. Even when they aren't, don't panic and don't reject any idea out of hand, either.

Suppose you ask Katherine, who recently returned to work from maternity leave, what you can do for her. She's quick to say you can make her work easier if you let her do all her work at home via computer and send it to you electronically.

Your first thought may be that she's asking for the impossible. After all, you need to have her in the office for spontaneous consultations and last-minute meetings, and you don't want to set a precedent. Before you say that, however, see if you can find a compromise.

One compromise may be a limited pilot project with both time and day limits. Perhaps Katherine can work at home Wednesdays for one month. At the end of that month, you could both evaluate the costs and rewards of the pilot project. Both of you will have to develop a set of specific criteria by which to evaluate the efficacy of the experiment and whether or not to continue.

As you iron out details of this compromise, it will become clear to Katherine that you will be incurring many costs in order to help her get part of what she wants. She should willingly go along with your change requests to compensate you for these costs and keep the relationship equitable.

Let's say that even the one-day-a-week experiment won't work for you at the present time. You may be able to find another solution if you explore why Katherine wants to be at home so much. Most likely she wants to spend more time with her baby and contain her day-care costs. Ask her if there are other ways to meet her goal.

Katherine may say that an infant day-care center in the building would allow her to spend at least her break time with the baby. You agree that this is a great idea, but you don't have the budget or the authority to institute such a program. You're a member of the executive board, however, and you do have the power to present such a proposal for approval. You can offer to spend your time, ideas, energy, and clout on this proposal for Katherine. These are all valuable rewards to Katherine and you can offer to trade them for changes on her part.

There are two catches here. The first is that you can't guarantee to Katherine that you will be able to win approval for this proposal. Make that clear, or Katherine may feel cheated when she makes the changes you've asked for and then finds out the proposal has been rejected.

The second catch is that you might be tempted to put less than your best effort into selling the idea to the executive committee, offering Katherine an insufficient "I tried" in return for her observable changes. This creates an inequity in the exchange. You must not only make your best effort, you must keep Katherine advised of your effort so that she can see for herself that you are upholding your end of the bargain.

DETERMINING THE VALUE OF YOUR RESOURCES

In addition to knowing what resources you control, you need to know their value to other people. The greater the value of the things you do for others, the greater should be the value of what they do for you. Several market factors affect the value of your resources.

Supply and Demand

The basic economic principles of supply and demand apply to interpersonal requests as well. These principles help determine the value of your resources and their consequent utility as resources in exchanges. Knowing the value of the resources you are offering lets you ask for changes of equal reward value.

When you assess other people's needs, also analyze the supply available to meet their needs. If many other people can meet their demands, your resources lose value. If, on the other hand, you're the only one around who can meet their demands, you can ask for more in return. While you may have a corner on the market, remember that your goal is equity in long-lasting relationships, not short-term profit by exploitation.

Sometimes we determine the value of the things we do for others in terms of how we would like it if it were done for us. This is a mistake. If you'd love it if someone would fine-tune all your written work, you might think you're offering Steven a big reward when you offer to edit and proof his quarterly market analysis. Steven might not want you to change a single comma. Conversely, while you think of an inside garage space as a minor benefit, your co-worker with the new Explorer might think it's a little piece of heaven.

The easiest way to determine the market value of your resources is simply to ask.

"Would that be of help to you?"

"Is that something you would really like me to do?"

Most people will give you a straightforward assessment of the value of what you have to offer. You can use estimated value to propose a trade that will be equitable and profitable for both of you.

Timing

The best time to make a request is when other people need things from you. This is when your resources have the greatest value. You can make trades equitably and profitably during these times of high need, but you have to use extra care in preparing your contingencies. Don't make the mistake of trying to gouge the other person. Your resources have temporarily increased in value but tomorrow things will return to normal.

Given these qualifications, a crisis may present just the opportunity you need to effect a change that the other person has been persistently resisting.

THE WORLD'S MOST PERSUASIVE COMMUNICATION

The basic tool for producing change is the IF-THEN contingency. As you begin to use this form of communication in your own requests, notice how it is used, and misused, by others.

When someone is trying to make a persuasive appeal, write down the exact IF-THEN contingency beneath their words. Next time you're stuck in a committee meeting, instead of daydreaming or doodling, write down the specifics of the proposals that people are making, keeping an eye out for the basic if-then elements.

Watch how George, who spent seven minutes detailing why his group wanted a new microwave for the

break room, gets shot down in thirty seconds, ostensi-
bly because the office budget won't stretch that far.
Then watch how smoothly Melanie wins approval for
her even more expensive request for three more fax
machines by describing exactly how the company will
save money and increase sales.

As you gain skill, watch to see if people clearly
specified the action they wanted. Notice too whether
they were specific about the rewarding consequences
in the THEN part of the contingency. You'll probably
notice that people often neglect the THEN reward.
They may describe what they want the other person to
do for them, but they hardly mention how the other
person will benefit.

Compare successful and unsuccessful pitches. Top
persuaders emphasize the tangible consequences the
other person will enjoy, if he'll go along with per-
suader's request. Less successful persuaders tend to
talk only in generalities about the attributes of what
they are offering, rather than spelling out the immediate tangible benefits the other person will receive.

You can enhance your persuasive skill by starting
with small requests for change from your co-workers
and subordinates. On another sheet of paper, write
down the specific action or actions you want to request
in the IF portion of your contingency. Next, write
down the specific benefits the other person will receive
when he does what you ask. Use your written contingency to begin privately practicing how you'll word
your change request.

After you use a contingency to make a request,
analyze why it succeeded or failed. Pay especially close
attention to those situations in which you encountered
resistance. Was there something in your contingency

that produced the resistance? Were you asking the person to do too much, or were you unclear about what exact action you wanted him to take? Were you offering resources that were truly valuable to the other person?

Making Trades

If you're not feeling very certain about your ability to make these trades, start small and build your skill and confidence with successful practice. You are generally in a high power position with your subordinates, so you may wish to initiate the trading process with a subordinate with whom you have a fairly good relationship.

As a staffer in the Training Department you manage, Annette is one of the five key people in your business life. Consult the list of changes you want from Annette and pick one. Next, review the list of requests Annette has made in the past few weeks. You know what you want, and have a good idea of what she'll come in and ask for. Practice saying your contingency aloud in private while you wait for her to come to you.

Annette enters your office with words of praise about the good ideas you always have, and then inquires whether you'd look over the materials she developed for her presentation on serving internal customers. During the weeks of monitoring her requests, you discovered she regularly asks to run things by you, which often results in your doing a portion of her work for her.

This time you're ready. "I'll tell you what," you say. "I still haven't received the complete inventory of all our A-V equipment and the list of training tapes I asked you for last month. If you'll get those lists to me by four o'clock today, I'd be glad to use the remainder of the afternoon to review your presentation with you. Okay?''

You've made your if-then request. Now quit talking and smile expectantly. If the exchange is equitable, Annette will probably quickly agree, and you'll be ready to try another exchange with a different subordinate. You can expand the circle of those you're exchanging with, trading for larger changes from subordinates, and beginning to make trades with peers, and soon, superiors.

As you expand the circle, you may encounter more resistance. Your prior history of success will give you experiences that will enable you to handle these more challenging encounters. The next exercises are designed to build your skill at identifying and coping with resistance.

IDENTIFYING RESISTANCE

You don't need binoculars to use the Guide to Resistance Tactics. You can see plenty with the naked eye. To hone your ability to recognize resistance quickly, watch the resistance tactics employed by the people around you.

Detach yourself from the situation to make a better analysis. Watch how these key people resist requests that other people make of them before analyzing how they resist your requests. If you try to analyze the resistance aimed at you, you'll be too caught up in the moment to practice your resistance-spotting skills. Instead, practice by watching how other people deal with one another until you can spot and name each resistance tactic as soon as it comes into play.

These observations will provide a database you can use when you analyze how they resist your requests. Again, make a list of the tactics they use with you. Do they use the same tactics with you as they do with other people, or do they reserve a special set of maneuvers to avoid your change requests?

Patterns

As you become sensitive to the forms of resistance and more skilled at identifying them, you may begin to notice that people not only rely on the same tactics, but that they use them in the same predictable sequences.

One manager found that when he discussed the deficiencies in Bette's performance, he could predict that she would begin with denial.

"That's not true. I don't do that."

When pressed further, she would then change the subject.

"Why are you bringing this up to me? Edith is way worse than I am. She does this kind of thing routinely."

Bette would then follow this with a string of three emotions—anger, silence, tears.

"This really upsets me. I can't believe you'd accuse me of such a thing."

The subsequent silence would be accompanied by a sullen face. The manager usually caved in about here, but if the silence didn't get him to drop the subject, Bette moved on to tears. The manager got to the point where he could time Bette through the entire seven-minute sequence.

Once you've tracked the resistance tactics favored by the key people in your world, review your list to hunt for patterns. If you know in advance which resistance tactics an individual is likely to use, you can prepare and rehearse the circumvention technique best suited to counter it.

Reacting to Resistance

On separate sheets of paper, note how other people react when faced with resistance tactics. Notice how frequently they play right into the resistor's hand by switching over from their request to the subject the resistor introduces. Watch how quickly people defend themselves when called a name, how fast they respond to argumentative comments, and how readily they launch into long explanations when confronted with endless questions.

After learning to recognize the ways other people commonly react to resistance, you'll be ready to scrutinize your own knee-jerk reactions. Try to remember how you've reacted in the past when each of your five key people have resisted your requests. Knowing in advance your own impulses will help you substitute effective circumvention techniques for ineffectual reactions.

TAKING YOUR FIRST STEPS

You may feel prepared at this point to run through the entire Six-Step Process with someone who has been resisting your attempts to make a change. If you don't, you can take it step by step to build your skill and confidence.

First, listen to the words people use when they criticize something about a good performer or friend. They usually praise the person first, reassure them of their value and friendship, and then address the issue of concern.

On the other hand, when people criticize the poor performance of someone with whom they don't have a close relationship, they are apt to begin with a global indictment of the entire person. These kinds of indictments invite the very resistance—defensive maneuvers and emotional storms—a change-maker must avoid.

These observations should demonstrate the usefulness of praise and the futility of indictments, and should encourage you to practice positive feedback. You don't have to have a contingency to do this. Just start making positive comments about people's performance until you are more comfortable doing so, and other people become accustomed to your commendations. Give yourself a daily quota. If you haven't been much of a praiser, you're likely to find that people are more friendly and responsive to you.

Next, prepare for a meeting in which you'll set the positive context for your request and propose your change contingency. Don't worry about circumventing resistance at this time, or even about getting the change you want. Concentrate on practicing and refining your skill at these two steps in the sequence.

What you'll discover by taking these first two steps is that they are easier than you anticipated. You may very well get the changes you wanted right then and there. With that success behind you, you can go on to polish your style and delivery in subsequent trials. If you encounter resistance, rather than change, you now have the opportunity to begin practicing the fine art of bambooing.

Bambooing

If you know what resistance tactics you are likely to encounter, you can practice bambooing as you take your morning shower, or ride to work. Form is not important at this point. Just offer a phrase of acknowledgment, and then restate your change contingency.

If this feels awkward, consider how you would sympathize with a friend who has a problem. Francis says he's really angry about the change in schedules. You say you can see that it is really disturbing to him. He may then elaborate on the problems it will cause him. You agree that those could be serious problems. You do this automatically with your friends. You just have to adapt it for use with resistors.

You may run into someone who has also read this book, and she'll tell you she knows you're bambooing, as if it's an accusation. Simply acknowledge her perceptive observation.

"Good for you. I guess I am bambooing. Let's just focus on my proposal. Now, if you'll . . . , then . . ."

As you become more skilled at acknowledging people's responses to your requests, you'll overhear people saying that you've changed. They're right. You have changed, and their positive reactions are one of the rewards that should encourage you to refine your skills even further.

Rewarding Yourself

Your increased effectiveness in handling problems will be the greatest incentive to continue building your skills. Along the way, you need some incremental rewards to encourage your small steps. Each time you try one of these exercises, give yourself more than just a pat on the back. Find some more tangible ways to both reward and motivate yourself.

You are essentially creating a change contingency for yourself. Each of the specific actions recommended in these exercises are the IF portion of your own contingencies. The reward is the THEN part. The reward can be anything you like doing.

As you construct your to-do list for each work day, note the items that you most enjoy doing. Use these tasks as your rewards. Let yourself do these things you enjoy only after you have completed one of the practice exercises in this book.

Talking to yourself, you might say: "When I have taken at least five minutes to write down the rewards and costs Al and I exchange, then I can take Luke for a cappuccino, and tell him about my new marketing idea." The toughest part of these self-directed contingencies is the enforcement. No cheating. It has to be, IF and only IF.

FINALE

Thousands of people have learned how to use the tools in this book to gain more control over their lives and their relationships. By practicing these skills, you will begin to enjoy the success these tools can produce.

Beyond the specific tools and techniques offered here, there is a deeper message implicit in this new approach to people and change. That message is that despite what traditional psychological theories assert, neither your behavior, nor anyone else's behavior, has to be a mere repetition of past patterns.

The optimistic perspective that guides this whole approach is that change is possible at any time in a person's life. You can change the leopard's spots, and even old dogs like you can learn new tricks. Change is not only possible, the tools you need to make changes are now in your hands. Why not start to use them?

Acknowledgments

My thanks and deep appreciation to the people, and institutions, who made this book possible.

To Marilyn Jellison for her intellectual acumen, her business savvy, and her encouragement.

To Patricia O'Toole for her continuing faith, assistance, and friendship.

To those who have supported me over the years: Richard Byrne, Lawrence Warner, Randi Freidig, B.J. Hatley, Hank Weisinger, and the USC Institute of Systems and Safety Management.

To the members and staff of The Executive Committee.

To the University of Southern California and its students.

To Barbara Dickson and Daphne Bien for their editorial assistance.

To Fred Hills for his vision and good judgment.

ABOUT THE AUTHOR

Jerald Jellison, Ph.D., is a professor of psychology at the University of Southern California in Los Angeles, where he teaches and conducts research. As president of the USC Federal Credit Union, he knows what it is like to build and run a multimillion-dollar business in challenging times. For the past fifteen years, he has conducted management training seminars and spoken to business professionals throughout the United States and the Pacific Rim.